Kahtahah

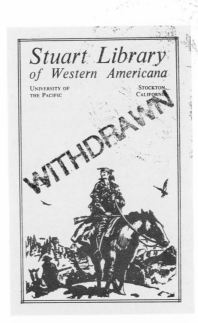

Kah

tahah

Frances Lackey Paul

**Illustrated by
Rie Muñoz**

ALASKA NORTHWEST PUBLISHING COMPANY
Anchorage, Alaska

Library of Congress cataloging in publication data
Paul, Frances Lackey, 1889-1970.
    Kahtahah.
    SUMMARY: Draws on the experiences of a real person to recreate the life of a Tlingit Indian girl of nineteenth-century Alaska.
    1. Kahtahah—Juvenile literature. 2. Tlingit Indians —Juvenile literature. [1. Kahtahah. 2. Tlingit Indians—Biography. 3. Indians of North America—Northwest coast of North America—Biography. I. Munoz, Rie. II. Title.
E99.T6P38 1976 970'.004'97 [B]   76-17804
ISBN 0-88240-058-4

Edited by Dorothy Jean Ray
Designed by Hilber Nelson

Alaska Northwest Publishing Company
Box 4-EEE, Anchorage, Alaska 99509
Printed in U.S.A.

contents

The story of Kah-tah́-ah is an attempt to recreate the life of a Tlingit Indian child for the pleasure of other children. It grew out of the desire of my own fourth grade Indian children in Juneau, Alaska, to read something about themselves. One day as we were reading about Indian children of the Southwest one of the boys asked me why no one ever wrote a story about the Tlingits.

Kah-tah-ah is my answer.

For the most part, Kah-tah-ah is a real person. Just such a little girl lived and played and adventured in the real land of the totem poles. As for her later life, her happy marriage lasted only four years, for in December 1886 her husband, also a Tlingit and named Yeil-eenuk, was lost with two others (Samuel Saxman, for whom the town was named, and another Tlingit whose name was Waak-kool-yud—farsighted one—named Edgar by the missionaries). The following spring, at the urging of Sheldon Jackson, Kah-tah-ah took her three little boys to Sitka to join the staff of what is now Sheldon Jackson College.

Kah-tah-ah became known and loved all over Southeastern Alaska, true to the old shaman's prophecy. The villages are filled with old men and women whom she nursed and mended, scolded and mothered during their childhood school days. In her ninetieth year she still brimmed over with life and love and interest in others. She is gone now.

The tribal system of these Indians is so complicated that ethnologists are content to use the name of their language as the name for the tribe and for the two clans, Eagle and Raven, into which they divided themselves.

There are some 40 autonomous tribes in each clan division. Each tribe owns its area of land where they reside, except for about three months in the winter beginning at the end of the fish season and ending just before the new run of fish is due. During this time they reside in communal villages but do not lose their autonomy. This led early white visitors to believe that such towns were integrated.

The Tlingit government is matriarchal. The head of each family is the mother's brother, the children follow the mother's clan and tribe, and in case of divorce, the mother takes the children. The names belong to the clan, so when a name is heard a person is immediately placed in his own separate niche, and those knowledgeable then know who the parents and ancestors are to the *nth* generation. A well-educated Tlingit doesn't have to ask an adult woman, Who are you? like the whites, because names are inherited.

While the clan name never changes, the tribal name often does. In this case, Kah-tah-ah's clan began as Raven and her ancestor's tribe as Git-sheesh, which is Tsimshian. This name became Kiks-uddi from an island called Kiks on which they settled. Because of an in-house fight for prestige Kah-tah-ah's tribe had to move. To shelter them, their brothers (they have no word for cousin) built a temporary shelter of yellow cedar bark; hence, they became known as Teehitton.

On the disability of her mother, Kah-tah-ah was raised by her aunt, Yutxoox ("x" is like the German "ch"), who would be called little mother, but in this case just mother.

"Snook" is shortened from Yux-ah-nusnook (bring him hither). Snook was chief of the migrants from "big house" on the Tahkoo (Taku) River a dozen generations ago, who camped on the Upper Stikheen (muddy water), now known as Stikine River. His emblem was the Eagle, a later name for the Wolf clan, and also indigenous to the "British side."

All of the information about Tlingit customs and folklore used in this story has been secured from original sources. In addition, I have checked all material with the publications of the American Museum of Natural History and the Smithsonian Institution, particularly with those of Lieutenant G. T. Emmons, Ret.

My sincerest thanks are extended to all my Indian friends who have so patiently told me stories of Indian life and answered my many questions about intimate details of the routine of living, as well as about the spiritual significance underlying the outward manifestations. It is my wish that these friends shall be satisfied with this effort to interpret their life in the symbols of the white man.

Most of all my thanks are to my husband, whose Tlingit name is Shquindy, shortened from Shkoon-idateeyee-kah (the man is honorable and therefore he will not do anything dishonorable). For without his help, his criticism and his interpretation, I am sure I should have become hopelessly involved in my attempt to recreate the primitive culture.

Frances Lackey Paul

Note: Frances Lackey Paul wrote her foreword in 1938, but material has been added to bring it up to date and explain the Tlingit tribal system. As an aid to pronunciation, hyphens appear in the names used in the foreword.

Kahtahah Goes to Summer Camp

Kahtahah *was a little Tlingit girl who lived in a village near the mouth of the Stikine (Stikheen, or muddy) River of Southeastern Alaska. She lived with her foster mother and foster father, Snook, the head chief of a great tribe.*

One morning she was awakened when her mother called out to her: "Kahtahah, wake up now! We are going to summer camp today. The large canoe is already loaded, and the sun will soon be shining."

Kahtahah sat up in her nest of squirrel robes and watched the women busily working around her. Some were packing food in boxes, some were taking down wall skins and storing them in carved red cedar boxes, and others were making bundles of clothing. All were talking and laughing because they were happy to go to the summer camp for the salmon fishing season.

Kahtahah's foster mother brought her a small piece of dried salmon. "Eat now," she said, "because who knows when the men will stop for food? But tomorrow night we'll have fresh salmon."

Kahtahah pulled on her moosehide moccasins with the baby seal fur edging. Taking the salmon her mother gave her, she ran down to the beach, singing, "We are going to summer camp! We are going to summer camp!"

Every family in the village was getting ready to go to its own summer camp. Dogs and children were everywhere, and the young men and slaves carried bundles down to the large, beautiful canoes, which were lined up on the shore, their protective skin and mat coverings removed. Each canoe was made from a single red cedar tree. Snook's canoes were painted with the Eagle design because Snook belonged to the Wolf clan, which has the eagle for its emblem. Some of the young men had their own canoes.

Kahtahah ran to her foster father, a tall, fine-looking Indian, but no longer young. She was his constant companion, and very dear to him. She stood quietly at Snook's side while his nephews brought down the last of the bundles and the loading was finished. The door of the Great House (where a chief lived with his family and the families of his sisters' sons) was closed but not locked, and when the salmon run was over they would return home to find that everything was just as they had left it. No Indian would steal.

The women, children and dogs got into the canoe. Snook helped Kahtahah to her place near him in the stern of the largest canoe, and the young men pushed it into the water. They leaped to their places and picked up their paddles. Everyone laughed and shouted. Summer had come!

In an hour all of the canoes belonging to the other Great Houses in the village were on the water and the winter village was deserted.

The Trip to Summer Camp

◆◆◆

They started early on a clear morning in May, the Leaf Moon Month, just as the sun rose in a pink and yellow glow from behind the sharp-pointed mountains of the mainland. Snook's summer camp was two long days' paddle away on one of the large islands toward the sea.

Kahtahah sat on a pile of blankets and chewed slowly on her dried salmon. None of the men had eaten breakfast because it was thought to be weak and womanlike to take food so early in the morning. On each side of the canoe were three men dressed in gay blanket coats made from Hudson's Bay blankets with striped borders. Kahtahah watched them dip their paddles in unison, the drops of water from their paddles turning to silver in the rising sun.

After traveling a long way across the wide water, the canoes came to another island, and Snook steered close to shore. Everyone stopped talking and the men dipped their paddles silently. A man in the bow of the first canoe lifted his gun. They soon neared the mouth of a little meadow creek. A small herd of deer—a buck, a doe and a small spotted fawn—came across the meadow and down to the beach to lick the salt seaweed. The man with the gun gave a shrill whistle and the deer stopped, their heads up, curious about the strange sound. The man shot. The buck leaped up, then fell to its knees, dead. The mother deer pushed the fawn back to the shelter of the trees and disappeared from sight by the simple trick of standing still.

The hunters killed just one deer because they needed food only for the journey. Everyone in the canoe began to laugh and talk, and Snook steered for the beach. The men jumped into the water and pulled the canoe high on the shore for their breakfast of fresh venison. One man began to skin the deer and others built a fire and unpacked the big cooking pots. Kahtahah ran up and down the beach with the other children looking for colored stones and shells.

The people gathered in a circle around the pots, which were lifted off the fires when the boiled venison was ready. Each person had a spoon made from a mountain sheep horn, so large that Kahtahah could eat but one spoonful. Everyone was tired of dried salmon and greedily ate the delicious stew.

When they had finished, bundles were quickly loaded into the canoes and they were on their way again, not to stop until they had reached the halfway point where they always camped overnight.

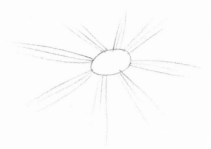

Arrival at Summer Camp

◆◆◆

Kahtahah curled up on her bundle of blankets and took a nap. She was almost 12 years old and taller than other Indian children of her age. Her hair, which was braided in two long, thick braids, had glints of red when the sun shone on it. Her foster mother carefully combed her hair every three or four days with a piece of comb that her real mother had given her.

Kahtahah was an Ahnyuddi (literally, "town," or high-caste) child, and was not permitted to do any of the rough work. Every head chief owned slaves taken in raids to the south or purchased from other raiders for the hard and routine tasks. Snook did not let her help smoke the fish, which would have stained her face, and Kahtahah's skin did not become as brown as that of the other Indian children, even in summer camp. Her hands were small and smooth— though often very dirty—and in winter her foster mother rubbed them with deer tallow to keep them soft.

The water of the wide channel was as smooth as Snook's copper shield before the Bear-with-ears-hanging-down had been carved on it.

The canoes made fast time since they traveled with the tide, and they drew up to their camping place an hour before sunset. There was plenty of time in the long twilight to cook their suppers and prepare for the short night. The sun went down in the northwest in a blaze of red clouds, an omen that rain would not fall while they slept. The next morning, with a light breeze, the large canoes raised mat sails woven of red cedar bark strips. To keep together, the large canoes towed the smaller ones, and they came to their own bay three hours before sunset. The summer village was situated at the upper end of the grassy meadows.

With the high tide, the canoes sailed smoothly through the pass at the head of the bay into a broad salt lake. Except at high slack or low slack tides, the pass was a raging rapids, a feature that had suggested the location of a summer village to Kahtahah's family long ago as a protection against surprise enemy attacks.

Both children and grownups were tired from sitting so many hours in the canoes and were glad to go ashore and move around. Some of the big boys went up to the creek with their fishing spears to get some early salmon or steelhead trout, and by the time the canoes were unloaded and the cooking fires started they had enough sockeye for a big feast of boiled salmon.

The last thing Kahtahah heard that night before she went to sleep was the far-off howling of a pack of wolves. Snook said, "There will be no deer here this summer. The wolves have driven them away."

Summer Camp

◆◆◆◆◆◆◆◆◆◆◆◆◆◆◆◆◆◆◆◆◆◆◆◆◆◆◆◆◆◆◆◆◆◆◆◆

The next morning everyone was busily repairing the camp for the summer. They put back the cedar shakes (hand-split shingles) that had blown off the roofs during the winter storms and straightened up the poles of the drying racks.

Bears often came down to the water from the woods through the tall dry grass of the meadows to catch salmon. One of the men had gone bear hunting in the meadows, and before the sun was halfway up in the sky, he returned, staggering under the weight of a fat young black bear. For their first breakfast in camp, everyone had juicy bear steak roasted over hot coals.

After she had eaten all she wanted of the strong red meat and had wiped her greasy hands on the dry grass, Kahtahah called to her sister Tsoonkla (dream mother): "Come on, let's go up to the creek and hide on the high bank. We might see a bear fishing."

They followed one of the bear trails up to the edge of the woods where the creek began to flow quietly through the meadows to the salt lake. They usually walked on the sand bars of the creekbed, but since they were still covered with water from the spring rains, they climbed up the bank. They picked their way quietly through the bushes to a high point overlooking a shallow pool, filled with splashing salmon, to watch the bears that often fished there. A blue jay began to scream over their heads, giving away their hiding place, but they no sooner were settled than they heard a crashing in the bushes on the other side, and a large black bear lumbered down the bank.

He immediately began scooping fish from the water with his forearm as swiftly as the lightning that flashes from the eyes of the legendary thunderbird. Kahtahah and Tsoonkla became so engrossed that they leaned far out, holding on to the berry bushes that grew at the water's edge. Suddenly, the bank, undermined by the high water, gave way and the two girls, berry bushes and all, fell into the pool almost on top of the bear.

"Woof!" said the bear, as startled as the girls, and took off in the opposite direction. The bear ran so fast that he had disappeared before they had even untangled themselves from the bushes.

Their fright over, the girls stopped running and began to laugh, now that they had already made so much noise that no more bears would come down to fish.

At the summer camp, Snook decided to have the bear hams cooked in a pit oven, a process that made the meat tender and juicy. When the girls returned they ran to the swamp and the beach to gather skunk cabbage leaves and seaweed for the roasting. The roasting pit was dug in the sand about three feet deep. Rocks, which had been heated in a big fire, were thrown on the bottom, then a layer of seaweed put over them. The bear meat was wrapped in the skunk cabbage leaves to protect it from sand, and laid on the seaweed. Another layer of seaweed and more hot rocks were placed on top, and the pit filled with sand. The meat was left to cook all night long in this first fireless cooker. Salmon and the hard little wild crab apples were also steamed in pit ovens.

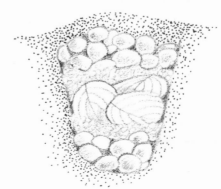

The wind changed to the southeast and the clouds blew in from the ocean, a sure sign of rain. This was the time when the tall dry grass that covered the meadows was burned off without danger to the summer camp, and within a week the meadows were soft and green again with fresh shoots.

Wild flowers were blooming all over the fields a month after they arrived, and as soon as the ugly brown bells of the wild rice appeared, Kahtahah and her foster mother dug up many plants— though only enough for one meal—with sharp digging sticks. They washed the little white kernels many times and soaked them in water all night to take out the bitter taste before cooking.

By this time the camp houses had been readied for sudden rainstorms. Drying poles were in place, alder wood was stacked near the smokehouses for the smoking fires and plenty of fresh food was on hand. It was time for a holiday. Everyone was happy and gay. They waded and swam in the warm water of the shallow streams that meandered through the meadows. They put down crab traps in the outer bay, and at very low tide made picnic trips to the adjacent bay to gather a special kind of black seaweed that was much prized for medicine. The young men raced and wrestled, but sometimes all were content merely to lie in the warm sunshine.

Spring Eulachon Camp

◆◆

One day as they were watching a big eagle swooping to the water for a fish, Kahtahah told her foster mother that she liked the summer camp best of all the places that they lived. "All winter it is dark and cold and rainy," she said. "Then spring comes and we go up the Stikine to the eulachon camp, but it is still cold. In summer camp there are no grizzly bears to be afraid of and there are so many different things to do, so summer camp is much the nicest."

The eulachon camp was where Snook's family always stopped for two or three weeks in the spring on the way up the Stikine to hunt grizzly bears and to gather spruce roots. There they fished for eulachon, a sort of needlefish smaller than a herring, commonly called hooligan. These fish came into the big rivers to spawn by the millions, sometimes before the ice was gone. Then the men had to set their nets of woven spruce roots through holes in the ice, but the nets were often carried away if the eulachon run came after the breakup of the ice and the big blocks of ice rushed down the river, sweeping everything before them. The men who went out in canoes to dip up the fish in their baglike nets were in danger, too. Only the spring before, one of the slaves had drowned when a cake of ice upset his canoe.

The Indians knew when a fish run was coming because great flocks of sea gulls followed the eulachon up the river, flying about, screaming, diving, swimming and fighting as they fed on the eulachon all day long. The women strung hundreds of the little fish on bark ropes, hanging them in the sun and the wind to dry, sometimes with a slow smoking fire under them.

The fish were so rich in oil that it dripped out while drying. But the most important part of eulachon fishing was trying out the oil, which was done in several steps. First, the fish were heaped in large piles until they were partially spoiled, which separated the oil more quickly. The fish were then put in canoes or big boxes, and water and hot rocks added. The water was kept boiling with additional rocks until all the oil from the fish had risen to the top. When cool, the thick grease was skimmed off and stored in wooden boxes.

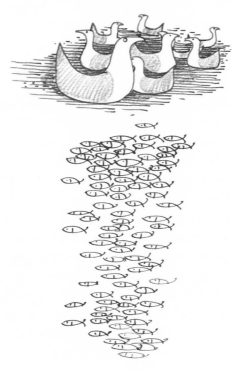

When the eulachon run was large all the Indians filled many boxes with grease. The Tlingits liked to use the oil themselves for dipping dried halibut and salmon and as a sauce for boiled salmon eggs, but they also traded it to Indians who did not own a spring camp on the Stikine. Good eulachon fishing grounds made rich Indians because others traveled long distances just to buy the oil.

How a Chief's Son Acquires a Name

◆◆◆◆◆◆◆◆◆◆◆◆◆◆◆◆◆◆◆◆◆◆◆◆◆◆◆◆◆◆◆◆◆◆◆

After their brief holiday, everyone began to work in earnest to lay in a supply of food for the winter. With every incoming tide the silvery fish came into the salt lake by thousands, and the young men piled fresh branches across the V-shaped mouth of the salmon trap. Sometimes the water seemed to boil with the salmon, which played around in the tidal streams back of the trap, leaping out of the water, twisting and turning and falling back with mighty splashes. The salmon were happy, the Indians said, because they liked the feel of fresh water, but when the tide turned and the fish followed the water running swiftly out, they were caught in the brush between the rock walls of the trap.

The men brought the catch to the beach at every tide, and the women cleaned and sliced them thin to dry on the racks for a day or two in the sun. They were then taken to the smokehouses where the constant alder wood fires gave the fish a nice sweet taste.

At first all the fish were bright silver, almost blue on their backs, but as they stayed near the fresh water of the creeks, they began to turn a dull red. Then Kahtahah knew that they were nearing their spawning time and would soon slip up the creeks on their way to the lakes.

Thousands of the rich red salmon were needed to feed Snook's house the next winter, but Kahtahah had no part in drying the fish since it was not considered suitable work for a chief's daughter. But she often watched the women at their cutting.

Thousands of the rich red salmon were needed to feed Snook's house the next winter, but Kahtahah had no part in drying the fish since it was not considered suitable work for a chief's daughter. But she often watched the women at their cutting.

One day Kahtahah picked up the knife of one of the women who had left her cutting board and tried to imitate her long, swift strokes. She knew well how to make all the cuts—even the notch near the tail with which to hold the slippery fish—and how to clean out the insides with one stroke of the knife, but she did not succeed very well. She found the squatting position uncomfortable. Both the fish and the knife were heavy and slippery, and the salmon bones were tough and the flesh soft. The knife constantly slipped and hit the wrong place so she made chopped-up hash instead of thin slices.

The women near her watched out of the corners of their eyes and chuckled at her struggles, but Kahtahah was so intent on her work that she was oblivious to them. Suddenly a hand fell on her shoulder and her foster mother's voice sounded above her. "Ee-ee! Ee-ee! What is this that you are doing? Look at your hands! I can't leave you for a moment without your disgracing yourself!"

Kahtahah dropped the knife and hung her head in shame. Her mother could not help smiling as she looked at the chopped-up fish, so she did not scold Kahtahah further, but Snook was very stern and talked to Kahtahah a long time about the responsibilities of her caste.

Once Kahtahah took a leisurely walk with her foster father all the way up the big creek to the lake. Snook shot a ptarmigan, which they roasted on a forked stick over a small fire for lunch. They discovered that a beaver dam, built across the mouth of the creek where it joined the lake, had lowered the water in the creek so that the fish could not reach the lake, and hundreds lay dying on the sand bars before they had spawned.

After they returned home, Snook sent slaves up the creek to break down the dam. "The beavers will have time to build other homes somewhere else before winter," he said. "We cannot let them spoil our salmon streams. The fish are more important to us than the beavers are."

Yes, fish were very important to them, and Snook told her one of her favorite stories about the fish people while they sat in front of their little fire at lunchtime.

"Many years ago, when Raven was still building the world, there was a large village named Dahxeit near Sitka (although some say it was near the marble quarry on Calder Creek). There the young boys played in and out of the nearby salmon stream, often snaring sea gulls, one of their favorite games.

"One day, the chief's son was very hungry after an unsuccessful chase for sea gulls. He yelled to his mother, 'I'm hungry. Give me something to eat,' and she gave him the bony shoulder piece of dried salmon. When the boy saw what his mother had given him, he asked scornfully, 'Why do you always give me the bony shoulder piece that nobody ever wants?' and flung it away.

"Just then the boys called to him: 'A sea gull is in your snare. A sea gull is in your snare!' His hunger forgotten, the chief's son rushed into the water to retrieve the snare and line, which the sea gull was pulling into deeper water. Farther and farther the sea gull pulled it, just beyond the boy's reach until the boy disappeared. He had been pulled under the water.

"In the water, on either side of him, appeared to be an army of men, all facing silently in one direction. Their huge eyes stared at him unblinkingly, and when they began to march, he went along with them.

"Time passed, but none of the people took any food although their mouths were constantly moving as if eating. 'But why can't I eat?' he thought, and looking down, saw what he thought were fish eggs. He wondered why they were not eating the eggs. 'We eat them at home. Why not here? I'll try to eat some when they are not looking,' he thought, and he scooped up a handful.

"They kept on marching, and when he thought nobody was looking, he slid some of the eggs into his mouth. Just then the salmon people yelled, 'Shunyuxklax has eaten our dung. Shunyuxklax has eaten our dung.' The chief's son was mortified, and thus he learned that a person must always speak respectfully about food and not insult it as he had done with the bony shoulder piece of the dried salmon. The salmon people gave him his Tlingit name, Shunyuxklax, which refers to that piece of salmon, and is a name you must remember, otherwise your old people will think that you are not educated.

"Shunyuxklax adjusted to life with the salmon people and had forgotten his human form until four years later when he became aware of a great movement in the salmon tribe. They began moving away, each one wanting to go to the stream of its birth. Thousands of them started onward, and as they journeyed, one or more would leap out of the water. When he asked why they did that, he was told that they were scouts.

"On the way they met an even greater number of smaller fish, which were silvery in color. They were hilarious with joy, and said they were on their way home, exclaiming, 'You're too late, too late. You had better go back. We have finished everything.' Shunyuxklax had never seen any creatures so crazy as they passed each other.

"On this journey, groups of his army would drop off, explaining, 'The stream to which we belong is this way,' and pointing to it, off they would go. This continued until Shunyuxklax arrived at his parents' stream, which was very wide and shallow, only a few inches deep in some places. On the bank where the houses stood, he saw a row of women squatting near the water's edge, cutting salmon for easy drying.

"After a while, his companions said to him, 'Your mother is over there. Why don't you go close to her?' Sure enough, he recognized his mother, but was afraid to go near and only sidled up, rushing suddenly away. Indeed, all of his companions edged up close to the women, a few even claiming that some of them had no petticoats on. That is why they rushed up close and then, with great laughter, rushed back to the opposite bank. But they continued to urge Shunyuxklax to go near his mother. She noticed him at last, and calling to her husband, said, 'Come here. There is a fine-looking young salmon that keeps coming close to me. Spear him so that we can have a nice roast salmon.'

"This frightened Shunyuxklax so much that he stayed away, but his companions said, 'Don't be afraid. The spear hurts only at first, and then a nice feeling will come over you, and you will be fine.'

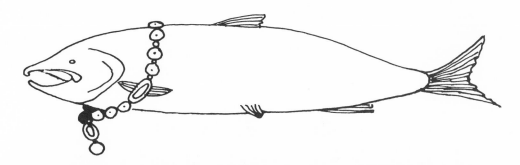

"At last the husband speared him and turned him over to his wife. She began cutting his neck with her shell knife, but it kept slipping and would not cut. She examined the edge of the knife and exclaimed, 'This salmon has a copper necklace. It looks like the one my son had on when he disappeared.' Her husband took the salmon, wrapped a mat around it and placed it on a board near the roof.

"That evening as the people sat around the fire, they heard someone singing. They looked outside but nobody was there—only the salmon lying on the mat. They went inside, and again heard singing. A brave man ran out to find out who was coming, and seeing the mat move, pulled the cover aside. There, instead of a salmon, lay the boy who had been missing for so long. He took the young man to his father and mother, and the boy told them everything that had happened to him during his long absence.

"His father then gave him the same name that the salmon tribe had called him, Shunyuxklax. He was known far and wide by this name, because he was the boy who was captured by the salmon tribe for insulting the precious food of the 'people who traveled along the tidal waters.'" From this comes their name, lein (the tidal area) git (people), usually spelled Tlingit.

How Raven
Fooled Seagull and Crane

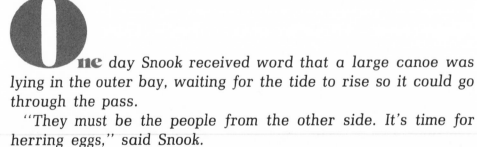

One day Snook received word that a large canoe was lying in the outer bay, waiting for the tide to rise so it could go through the pass.

"They must be the people from the other side. It's time for herring eggs," said Snook.

The big canoe came slowly into the salt lake when the tide had ceased to roar through the rocky pass and the waters ran slack. In it was a trading party from the seaward side of the big island where the herring ran thick in the spring. They wanted to get eulachon oil and brought many dried herring eggs to trade. Snook had plenty of eulachon oil so he took all the herring eggs the visitors brought, and they went happily away.

When the herring swarmed in from the ocean, these westward people had cut down hemlock trees to put into the water for the spawning fish. Millions of tiny white eggs were caught on the branches, which were then taken out to dry in the wind and the sun.

To eat the eggs, the branches were soaked in water until the
eggs slipped off. Then the eggs were boiled a very short time until
they were like transparent seed pearls. Kahtahah liked to eat
herring eggs because of the fresh salty taste and the crackly noise
they made between her teeth.

The chief had been right when he said that there would be no
deer near the summer camp because the wolves had driven them
away. Not once all summer long did the hunters see a deer track
along the beaches and the creeks. Whenever they needed
venison, the young men had to hunt across the channel on another
island where there were no wolves. The meat that was not used at
once was cut into thin strips and dried and smoked. The tallow
was mixed with berries and poured into skin bags for winter use,
and the skins were tanned and bleached, sometimes as white as
the blossoms of the crab apple trees, for clothing and moccasins.
The old women sat constantly at the stretching frames, scraping
and softening the skins with their dull bone knives.

Kahtahah, already a skillful seamstress, was making herself a
white deerskin dress with bead trimmings. She had a shiny needle
that had belonged to her real mother and some bright beads that
Snook had traded for furs from the Hudson's Bay Company. As
Kahtahah sewed, she watched two old black ravens strutting
back and forth on the ridge of the smokehouse, talking to each
other.

"They sound like two old men," she said. "I wonder if they are
talking about the salmon in the smokehouse. Ravens are greedy,
but they are lazy, too. Mother, tell me the story about how the

raven tricked the sea gull and the crane." She told the following story as they sewed.

"Raven walked along the beach one day, hungry. The water bubbled with a big school of herring, but Raven, though a fish eater, was no fisherman, and he had to find a way to get a herring. He looked around and saw a crane standing on one leg in the water, fishing, and a sea gull that had just lighted on a rock after swallowing a nice, fat herring. He could see the big bulge that the herring made on the side of the sea gull's breast and said to himself, 'I must have that herring or I'll die.'

"He walked past Crane and spoke to him, and then strolled over to Seagull. Returning to Crane, he said, 'I don't like to tell you this, but I feel that I ought to because I am your friend. You saw me talking with Seagull. He called you an ugly, long-legged brute and said that your ancestors were slaves.' Crane did not answer.

"So Raven walked over to Seagull and asked, 'You saw me talking to Crane just now? I really don't like to do this, but I feel that I should because I am your friend. That Crane called you some very insulting names; said you were a no-account, a common thing of low birth, and that your grandmother was a witch.' Seagull said nothing.

"Raven then walked back to Crane and whispered, 'I think I had better warn you that Seagull just told me that he was coming over here to fight you. If he does, just remember that his weak spot is his chest. Kick his chest hard and you will win the fight.' Crane looked over at Seagull, who acted restless. He felt grateful to Raven.

"Raven then went to Seagull. 'I wonder,' he asked, 'what is the matter with Crane? He seemed so angry at you, kept calling you insulting names, and just now told me that he was coming over here to give you a beating. You had better not wait. See him looking at you? You had better start right out and if he tries to kick you, stick your chest at him and he can't hurt you. You go at him hard with your chest.' Just then Crane shifted from one foot to the other. 'See that? See that?' Raven exclaimed. 'He is planning to come at you. You had better start at him right now.'

"So Seagull and Crane started toward each other, grateful that their good friend Raven had warned them and prepared them for victory. They walked faster and glared at each other as they approached. Both fairly flew the last few feet. Remembering the good advice Raven had given him, Crane raised his foot and kicked at Seagull's chest with all his might, and Seagull, having been warned by his good friend Raven, promptly presented his chest to receive the blow. Crane struck, and the herring popped out. Raven caught it before it fell into the water, and flew off chuckling. Crane and Seagull realized that Raven had told them a bunch of lies and stopped fighting. When our people hear stories that make them feel angry toward others they say, 'Perhaps Raven is carrying tales to Seagull and Crane once more.' Everybody understands what is meant.''

Kahtahah laughed. ''Raven was always playing tricks on people, wasn't he, mother?''

''Yes,'' she answered, ''but Raven was kind to us, too.''

Seals

◆◆◆

The hair seals had a rookery on a small rocky island without trees or small bushes out in the channel near the mouth of the bay. The seals talked together a lot—the old ones with hoarse grunts and growls and the young ones with shrill squeals and whistles—and Kahtahah used to pretend she could understand what they were saying to each other. Hunters had to be skillful to get a seal at the rookery, even though they came close in a small canoe and imitated their growls, because the seals were very sensitive and dove into the water, leaving the rock bare, at the slightest disturbance.

The seals liked to eat salmon and often took just one bite out of a big fish, dropping it to seize another. They sometimes followed the salmon up to the salt lake, where the hunters shot them right in front of the camp. All of the skins were tanned for rugs and moccasins, and the thick layer of seal blubber was cut into pieces and melted over a slow fire. The oil was stored for winter in many wooden boxes in every house. Blueberries, highbush cranberries and crab apples were also preserved in this oil.

One of the women had been working very hard for weeks with her seal oil. Her boxes, sitting in a row in front of her smokehouse, were full, but they had no covers. She had asked her husband to make new covers ever since they had arrived in camp, but he was lazy and did not want to make them. One day the wind felt like rain, and to prevent water from getting into her seal oil, she again asked him to make the covers, but he just sat on a rock on the beach without bothering to answer.

She watched him as long as it takes to count 25, then picked up a large box of thick, sticky oil and turned it over his head. Alarmed at the wickedness of her act, she waited only a second, then ran up to the woods to hide.

The box reached down to his shoulders, and the oil ran all over him. Everyone roared with laughter, Snook so hard that he could not stand up. Some of the women ran to help the poor man, who would have smothered to death in the sticky oil if they had not pulled off the box. They brought handfuls of moss to wipe the oil from his face, his eyes and even his ears.

He did not say a word, but just sat there for a long time. Finally he got up, and going into the smokehouse, he picked up a smooth piece of cedar wood and his adz and began to shape covers for the oil boxes. He seemed to think they would present less danger to him with the covers on.

Box Making

◆◆◆◆◆◆◆◆◆◆◆◆◆◆◆◆◆◆◆◆◆◆◆◆◆◆◆◆◆◆◆◆◆◆◆◆◆◆◆

Snook decided that he needed more boxes because many good ones had been traded along with the eulachon grease, and he thought there would not be enough left for their own supplies. Most of the new boxes were made of hollowed-out logs, but some were bentwood boxes, the body of which was made of only one long piece of thin wood.

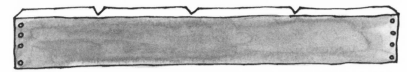

Snook himself chose the tree for these boxes. On one of his rambles with Kahtahah, he had found a red cedar tree with a straight trunk and few branches and marked it with a blaze. A couple of young men returned to cut it down and to split off thin boards from the logs.

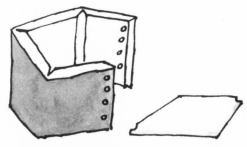

Making boxes was exacting work. Only the most skillful workmen could make good boxes of bentwood. In camp, the boards were cut into the right size and shape, and a small groove was cut in each board for three of the corners. Holes punched at the two ends formed the fourth corner when joined with bark or sinew thread. The thin boards were bent by steaming over water that was kept boiling with hot rocks. When soft they were taken out and carefully bent at the three grooved corners so as not to break the wood, and the ends were sewed together. The bottom was sewed on in the same way. Snook would carve designs on the best boxes during the winter.

Kahtahah had a very beautiful small box that Snook had made for her when she had the coughing sickness (tuberculosis) one winter. The box, with a raven carved at one end and a frog at the other, was made to hold a necklace of carved bones which the shaman (medicine man) had given her. The eyes of the raven and the frog were inset pieces of abalone shell, and the top was bordered with opercula. The rest of the box was stained black and was so highly polished that it shone like the black stones that made the fire burn so hot.

Kahtahah had been very sick the winter her real mother died of the coughing sickness, and Tsoonkla, her sister, had gone to live in the Teehitton (barkhouse people) house. Kahtahah was so sick that she had spit blood, and Snook, afraid that she, too, would die, took her to Shquindy, the shaman, who was Kahtahah's own uncle. He was a great shaman, and so powerful that he would cure nobody without pay, not even his own niece. Snook had sent blankets to him as payment when he took Kahtahah to Shquindy.

Shquindy knew that they were coming and had prepared for their arrival by fasting for two days. He had drunk nothing but salt water, which he spit out in long streams. Snook carried the little sick child in his arms and laid her on the mat before the shaman, who sat in the seat of honor against the back wall of his house, with his rattle carved in the shape of a land otter in his hand. Shquindy was a fearful creature. His hair, which had never been cut in his whole life, was long and matted. His skin, very white and clear, was tightly drawn over the bones of his face, and though his eyes were sunk deep into his head, they were very sharp and bright. Kahtahah was sure they could look right down into the heart of a little girl, and straight through the bones of her head to read the thoughts that filled her mind. He was very thin from frequent fasting when he was making medicine. Kahtahah was afraid of Shquindy, even though he was her uncle, normally a very close relationship among the Tlingit people.

At the crown of Shquindy's head was a lock of white hair. In the raven blackness of his hair, this piece had once been brown, but in his old age it had become pure white, the rest of his hair remaining black. Many years later Kahtahah had a little boy of her own with a lock of white hair at the crown of his head. She named him Shquindy.

A drum was beating in the corner of the big room where Shquindy sat chanting one of his medicine man songs softly to himself. In his youth, he would have run around and around the center fire until his "yake" (spirit) took possession of him, but lately he had made just as strong medicine by chanting to himself.

Kahtahah lay shivering on her little mat. Sometimes the shaman looked at her with his fierce eyes, but most of the time he looked off into space, seeing neither Kahtahah nor the crowd that filled the room, swaying in time to the beat of the drum, and hearing nothing but the sound of his own rattle and chant.

Finally, with a fierce shake of his land otter rattle, Shquindy stood up. The people held their breath. He took a necklace of queerly shaped small bones, brown and shiny from age, out of his big box of charms and fastened it around Kahtahah's neck. Then he chanted in the singsong tones of the shaman, "This child shall not die. She will become a woman. She will live to an old age. She has work to do among her people. The Tlingit will love her. She will be known among them from the north to the south, from the mountains to the sea. She bears a noble name. Her name means 'highly esteemed.' It is a man's name. This child will be highly esteemed among the Tlingit. Shquindy has spoken."

The old shaman dropped to the ground and sat with his head sunk on his breast. Snook picked up Kahtahah in his arms and carried her back to his house. Everyone believed Shquindy's words, and did not treat Kahtahah like a sick child from then on. She stayed out of doors all day, ate plenty of good food and drank a lot of seal oil and eulachon grease. The coughing sickness was soon gone, and never again did Kahtahah spit blood. The old shaman, her uncle, had made strong medicine.

The Story of the Grizzly Bear

Kahtahah did not mind rainstorms because she would sit in the smokehouse by the slowly burning alder fire listening to her foster father's stories. She like best the story of Snook's fight with the grizzly bear, which he always acted out. Snook almost died during that fight and Kahtahah knew that it was partly her fault, though it had happened when she was too small to remember.

Snook, who had always been very strong, was a famous grizzly bear hunter. At the time of this encounter, his people were camping in bear country on the banks of the Stikine on Snook's own tribal property. Kahtahah had been his favorite ever since she had come to him, and she went everywhere except grizzly bear hunting with him. That was too dangerous. She cried to go along that time, so hard that she finally fell asleep. Snook and his nephew slipped away so quickly that Snook forgot to take his short hunting spear.

In the woods, his nephew stopped to knock some pitch gum, which the Tlingits love to chew, from a spruce tree, and Snook went on with his small dog. In a small clearing, Snook saw a grizzly lying on its back as if dead. He watched it for some time while his little dog barked and ran up to it, but the bear did not move. The bear, however, quivered when the dog bit its paw, so Snook knew it was only playing dead. Grizzlies are very smart.

Snook then changed his position so that he could kill it with one good shot, because he did not have his short spear. Just as Snook stooped under a short jack pine, the bear, as if having planned it, leaped toward him. Snook, turning to defend himself, shot at close range, but the bullet must have passed under the bear's forearm because the bear was upon him at once. To save himself, Snook grabbed its short ears, the only place he could catch hold of.

Snook was a powerful man. He backed the bear into the open swamp and reached for his big hunting knife that he carried in his belt. In his struggle, the hunting shirt made of a blanket had slipped over his knife, and time and again, Snook tried to pull it out, but always failed because of that blanket coat. Then, with lightning speed he had to put both hands back on the bear's ears.

The bear then began to shove Snook about, back, back, past small trees and around holes until Snook became a very tired man. The bear would raise its head and blow its fierce hot breath into Snook's face, and he would muster all his strength to pull down the bear's head. Snook would jam his leg into the bear's mouth with such strength that the bear could not close its jaws, but Snook knew that he could not continue. Blood ran from the wounds on his chest and legs made by the bear's claws and teeth, and he was tired and weak. With his remaining strength Snook managed to back up to a large log, five or six feet thick, and with one last effort, pushed the bear away and threw himself over the log. With this last leap, Snook lost consciousness.

When he awoke, his nephew was washing his face with cold water and the bear lay dead on the other side of the great log. Snook's wounds healed, but he was never again as strong as before. He became known as the Man-who-fought-with-a-grizzly and made up a dance about the fight to dance at the great feasts. He then showed the bear's skin with ears like a dog's, which Snook had stretched with his own hands in the struggle for his life.

The Story of the Village of Gidiksh

◆◇◆◇◆◇◆◇◆◇◆◇◆◇◆◇◆◇◆◇◆◇◆◇◆◇◆◇

Kahtahah also liked to hear Snook tell the story about the village of Gidiksh, where there had been a war a long time ago. The enemy had burned the village and killed all the people except the chief's sister and her little girl, who lay hidden. When the enemy left, the mother and child found refuge among the people of her own tribe in another village.

As the girl grew up, her mother began to plan for her marriage. She had never forgotten the death of her relatives, and deep in her heart she dreamed of raising a family and rebuilding Gidiksh.

To carry out her plans, she sat down at the edge of the village and sang over and over, "Who will marry my daughter? She is young. She is beautiful. She is well trained. Who will marry my daughter?"

After a time a strong, handsome man came to her and said, "I hear that you wish to have a husband for your daughter. How would I do?"

"What can you do?" she asked.

"I am a powerful man, the most powerful in all the land. The earth trembles when I roar," and roar he did, and tore up trees by the roots.

The mother feared that he might not be kind and gentle with her daughter so she said, "No, you will not do." When he turned and lumbered off she saw by his walk that he was a bear.

Another handsome young fellow came and offered himself. In answer to the mother's question, he said, "I am the swiftest runner in all the land. There is no one as swift as I."

But the mother shook her head, and when the young man went bounding away into the woods, she saw that he was a deer.

Still another, strong and handsome in his white coat, came asking for the hand of her daughter. "I fear no one," he said. "I live high in the mountains where I am the great chief." Again the mother said, "No, you will not do." He was a mountain goat.

Shortly after this another man came swiftly and sought the young maiden's hand, saying, "I am strong, and besides, I am smart. I am known as a great hunter." He was a wolf. He ran out and quickly returned with the mountain goat slung over his shoulder. But none of this pleased the mother.

All of the animals came. The frog said, "I am small, but even the big animals are afraid of me." The mink said, "I have a peculiar smell that frightens away all other animals." The wild canary said, "I am the sweetest singer." The fox said, "I wear the most beautiful clothing and am cunning." All claimed the hand of the girl, even the rabbit, the squirrel and the owl, who said, "To-hoo! To-hoo! Even men fear me when I call in the nighttime."

But none of the suitors satisfied the mother, and she said to all of them, "No, you will not do." As she continued to sit and sing, she thought, "I must marry my daughter to a good and brave man," and she knew that if she would only wait, the right man would come.

Suddenly there was a great clap of thunder, and a bright and shining being appeared, standing on the top of a mountain. The mother went close to him and asked, "What do you want?"

"I hear you have a daughter and I have come to seek her in marriage. I am the child of the sun. I move as quickly as light. I go wherever I wish as quickly as thought. I am never discouraged, and my strength increases with danger."

In her heart the mother knew that this was the man and said, "You may have my daughter."

A great round cloud came down from the sky and covered the child of the sun, the mother and the daughter. As it lifted them up the Shining One said, "Do not look. Keep your face hidden." But as they passed through the clouds there was a great noise and the mother opened her eyes. All of them fell back to earth. The Shining One said, "We will try once more, but if you open your eyes I must leave you behind."

The cloud lifted them a second time, and again they heard a great noise and the mother opened her eyes. They fell back to earth once more.

The child of the sun was angry. He said to the mother, "I cannot take you to my home in the sky. I must leave you here." He tore off a branch of a tree, pushed her into the hole and replaced the branch, saying, "You shall live here forever and be called Woman-of-the-forest. You shall cry whenever the wind moves the trees." That is why you hear the moaning of the trees whenever the wind blows.

Then the great round cloud lifted the child of the sun and his young wife through the air. She kept her face hidden as he had ordered, and when he told her to open her eyes, she was in a beautiful country filled with flowers and fruits. There they lived for many, many years, and had seven sons and one daughter.

One day the Shining One said to his wife, "I must go to a far country and may never come back, but you have your children and I will prepare everything so that you will never be in want. You will have enough. After a while you will want to go back to the old village where your brothers and your uncles used to live."

The mother had been thinking that she should go back to her old home. "The blood of my dead brothers calls me; the uncles of my children are calling them." She said nothing, but allowed the child of the sun to leave her.

When her sons were older, one of them came to her and asked, "Mother, who are we and where do we come from?"

She answered, "Go away and keep on with your playing," and he went away at once.

As the years passed, the young boys often asked the same question. They always received the same answer, and always went back to their games, but one day they said, "We will not leave you until you tell us who we are and where we came from." Then their mother knew it was time to tell them about the village of Gidiksh. When she finished her story the boys said, "Let us go back to the land of our grandfathers and our uncles and rebuild our town."

But the mother said to this, "No" and the boys went back to their games.

At last came a time when the boys did not ask their mother, but said instead, "Mother, we have decided to go back to Gidiksh and rebuild our town."

The mother then knew it was time for all to return to the land of their forefathers.

Their grandfather, whose name was Kagahn (the sun) built the children a small house with a painted front and a picture of the spirit of the sea, which was near their village, over the doorway. He filled 40 boxes with every kind of fruit and berry, dried salmon and eulachon grease, and put them in the little house. He gave bracelets and a marten robe to the girl because she was a chief's daughter and prepared war clothes, clubs and spears for the boys.

To his son's wife Kagahn said, "You and your children are going back to your village in the earthland where you will face great dangers. You may have to fight against great odds, but if ever your enemies become too strong for you, or if you should be in great danger or need, think of me and I will come to your help. I will not fail you if you call upon me."

At last all was ready. The mother and her children went inside the little house, and the great round cloud covered them and carried them down to their old home. There, amid the ruins of the old houses and the broken-down totem poles, the little house became a Great House with a painted front. The boxes of berries and other food turned into huge painted boxes. Everything that was small in the land of the sun became large in earthland.

They did not have a fort, so during the night they built the great fence around their house so that their ancient enemy would not learn of their presence until they were ready. However, people in passing canoes sometimes saw dark shadows moving about the old village. They reported this to the old enemy chief, who always answered, "These are the spirits of the dead who have come back. They are not happy because they were defeated in battle."

The seven brothers became impatient when they were nearly done and began working in the daytime. The passing canoes then saw real live persons in the old village and carried the news to the enemy chief. He ordered out his war canoes. "This time," he said, "I will destroy every one of them and will scatter their ashes to the winds."

When the children of the sun saw their ancient enemy approaching, they put on their war clothes and took up their war clubs and spears, ready for battle. They rushed into the water waist deep and formed a solid line of defense, swinging their war clubs and shouting encouragement to each other. Their mother and young sister stood on the beach behind them, hurling insults at the enemy, "Witches! Beggars! Slaves!"

The three big war canoes slowly pushed back the brothers, but they always kept their line so they would not be divided. They were finally pushed back to their painted house. The enemy's canoes were beached, and the warriors gathered to attack. From early morning until midday the unequal fight went on. The brothers were badly wounded, one by one, and remained behind the shortened line until each could gather enough strength to return to the defense. The women constantly shrieked defiance at the enemy.

It seemed that all was lost. Each brother was wounded and bleeding, and the line was tottering. Then a cloud seemed to drift across the sun. The mother remembered what her husband's father had promised. "Will he keep his word and come to our aid?" she thought. Why had she waited so long!

Lifting her face to the sun she cried, "Oh, that it were true, this thing that you promised me—that if I ever needed you, you would help me. Come, or we shall die."

The echo of her words had not yet disappeared when the sun shone with a wonderful light and power. All clouds faded from the sky, and the heat beat down with a terrible intensity. It seemed as

if the sun were alive. The war canoes cracked loudly, and the enemy warriors began to pant with thirst. Sweat flowed freely.

"Hoo-hoo-hoo-hoo-hoo-hoo-hoo," sang the brothers, who forgot their wounds and once more lifted high their weapons. The enemy, alarmed, fell back. The boys pursued them, killing as they went. The sun shone fiercer and fiercer until the eyes of the enemy were blinded. They rushed to the beach and plunged into the water. Those who reached their canoes found them cracked and useless.

The children of the sun went into the water, killing with every swing of their clubs until none of the enemy was left. They then went back to their great painted sun house, chanting a victory song. They continued to live there in peace and safety. The sister had many daughters, and in time they again became a great nation.

Snook always ended the story by warning the children never to make fun of or despise their enemies or they might be like those of Gidiksh. He also pointed out how wise the mother had been in the choice of a good husband for her daughter. That is why Tlingits of good family are so careful about the marriage of their daughters. Whenever the old people wanted to teach their children to plan wisely and to be brave and strong even when the way was hard, they always told the story of Gidiksh.

Kahtahah and the other children learned their history and folk tales from stories that the old people told them. This was their school, especially as they sat around the center fire in the long winter evenings.

Bears Like Blueberries

◆◆◆◆◆◆◆◆◆◆◆◆◆◆◆◆◆◆◆◆◆◆◆◆◆◆◆◆◆◆◆◆◆◆◆◆

The women and children had spent all morning picking blueberries from the low bushes at the edge of the forest. To pick the berries, each person placed a broad, flat basket on the ground under a bush and pulled down the branches, stripping them bare of both leaves and berries. She then shook the basket and blew all of the little sticks and leaves away, leaving the clean berries, which she emptied into a deep basket under the trees.

When Kahtahah carried her deep basket to the edge of the stream where many others stood ready for the canoe trip back to camp, she saw a mother bear and her two round, fat cubs tipping over the baskets, scooping the berries into their mouths, pawful after pawful.

"Look, Mother! Look, Tsoonkla! Oh, look, everybody! The bad wicked bears are spoiling our berries!"

All of the women came running to her call. Kahtahah was angry and wanted to run out and chase the bears away, but her foster mother pulled her back.

"Be quiet!" she warned. "Don't you see that it's a mother bear? We must be careful because even a black bear mother will fight for her cubs."

"But our berries will be gone!" cried the children.

"And our baskets, too!" the women exclaimed as the two cubs began to pull on the same basket. Both hung on tenaciously, squealing and growling. The mother bear, alerted by the noise, reached out with her big paw, and with one blow ripped the basket in two. The little bears tumbled over backward, but recovering, sat up on their haunches and looked at the other baskets. They rolled their naughty little eyes at each other, and as if propelled by one thought, scrambled to the other baskets, and imitating their mother, ripped them to pieces right and left.

Remembering the hunting stories her foster father had told her, Kahtahah said, "Come on. We must get the wind behind us. Snook told me that's the way to frighten black bears away. When they get our scent, the mother bear will tell her cubs to run into the woods."

Everyone stepped back into the trees and ran quickly over the soft moss to the other side where the wind would carry their smell to the bears. They peeped out from behind the tree trunks to watch.

The mother bear lifted her nose, sniffed the gentle breeze and thought, "Man-smell." Lumbering over to her cubs, she slapped

them away from their game of ripping berry baskets, and they disappeared into the forest so quickly that Kahtahah could not believe her eyes.

After a few seconds the women and children hurried across the meadow to the stream. Blueberries, mashed and spoiled, were scattered everywhere on the grass, and the baskets were badly torn.

"Ai-ee, ai-ee, those bad bears," sighed Kahtahah's mother. "Now we'll have to weave baskets all winter to replace them."

"I'm sorry I didn't eat every berry I picked," Tsoonkla grumbled. Kahtahah looked at Tsoonkla's berry-stained lips and teeth, and couldn't help laughing. "It's plain that you ate a lot at that," she answered.

"Those little black bears looked so cute when they tumbled over backward," Tsoonkla whispered. "I wish we could have them for pets."

Kahtahah answered, "It would be like the deer we had once. You remember how sweet it was when it was a little spotted fawn, but when its horns got big it tried to kill that boy who teased it and Snook said we should let it go before anyone was hurt. Snook would have had to make big presents if someone had been hurt. I cried under my blanket when they took my deer into the woods."

They picked up the baskets that could be mended, each woman hoping that she had enough spruce roots drying to make all the new baskets she would need.

How the Stikheenquan Came Down the River

◆◆

Who made the first basket?'' Kahtahah asked a few days later as she and her foster mother sat on a grassy bank in the summer camp, working on spruce roots. Coils of roots, which they were splitting into thin, flat strips, were soaking in a box of water in front of them. Wet roots did not break while being split.

"The first basket was made before the beginning of things-as-they-are," said her mother. "A cloud woman had married the sun. She and her children lived in the sunland for a long time, but she grew homesick and could think of nothing but how to get back to her old home on earth with her children. One day she pulled up some spruce roots and began to twist them together without really thinking what she was doing. The roots took the form of a basket.

"When the sun saw what she had woven he made it grow large enough to carry the cloud woman and her children down to earth. They came down in the Yakutat country and that is why the Yakutat women were the first to make baskets."

"Is that why you make such perfect baskets, mother?" laughed Kahtahah.

"Do not laugh at the old stories, my daughter. My Yakutat grandmother taught me all the different kinds of weaving and patterns. I didn't think I would ever weave a coarse work basket again, having left all that to the slaves, but now that the bears have torn so many baskets we shall have to weave together."

"Will you teach me another kind of weaving this winter?" Kahtahah asked. She loved to weave and had made her first flat blueberry basket all by herself when she was only eight years old. Her fingers were very nimble in twisting the many strands of roots in and out, following the designs her foster mother had taught her.

The women had gone into the nearby mountains to gather spruce roots early in the spring when the men hunted grizzly bears up the Stikine, but Kahtahah was not allowed to do any part of the digging. It was not considered suitable work for an Ahnyuddi child. The women dug in the shallow dirt with their hands and digging sticks, following each rootlet sometimes as far as 50 feet. The spruce roots were best in the spring when the thin outside bark was easily stripped off and the color was even. When the women got back to camp they held their coils of roots over hot coals until the outside bark was charred. They removed it by pulling each rootlet through a crack split in a stick. The roots were ready to split and dry after hanging all summer in camp.

Natural dyes were used for the blue, black, red and brown colors in the baskets. Blueberries made a dark blue color, and hemlock bark boiled with black clay from the sulfur springs made black dye. The inside bark of the alders used for smoking made orange-red dye, and the stems of the five-finger ferns made a rich brown.

The work of splitting had to be carefully done because a perfect basket could be made only with flat, even strips. For splitting they used knives made from steel files obtained from the Hudson's Bay Company in trade for many beaver skins. Before the white traders came the women used the sharp edge of a bone or a rock to split the roots, but they liked the steel knives better.

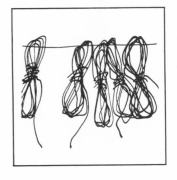

"For my new basket I shall use the sea wave pattern," her foster mother said. "That is an old, old pattern, older than the memory of the oldest grandmother. It shows something precious rising and falling on the waves."

"Maybe it tells the story of how we came to the Tlingit country," Kahtahah suggested.

"Oh, no. That is not the way the Tlingit came to this land," her mother answered.

"It's the way my sister Tsoonkla and I came," Kahtahah insisted. "But how did the oldest ones really come?"

"It is said that they came under the glacier that covered the whole of the Stikine in the very olden days. They were very brave people, those oldest ones.

"The story of their arrival comes to us from the grandmother of all grandmothers. In those days the Tlingit had traveled many weary days' marches through long grass that cut and bit deep into their legs. When they came to the headwaters of the rivers, some *of the people followed the streams down to the deep waters, some came down the Nass River, some down the Unuk, our people down the Stikine, some down the Taku and the Chilkat, some down the Alsek, and last of all, down the Copper River.*

"Some stayed at the mouths of the rivers, but others went farther out among the islands, even to the ocean itself. Some of your own family went many, many miles, clear to the Smoking Mountain [Mount Edgecumbe] near Sheet-kah [Sitka]."

"But how did the oldest ones know they could go under the glacier?" Kahtahah asked.

"I call them brave because they faced the unknown," her foster mother answered. "They camped at the glacier place for a long time and could see that the stream disappeared under the ice. That was all they knew. Finally an old man and his wife said, 'We are old. We have lived our lives. Give us a canoe and we will go under the ice to see what is there.' So the people gave a feast and a dance for the dead and the old man and woman started down the stream while the people sang a song still remembered by us.

"The shaman made medicine the whole time they were gone, and his spirit told him that the old people had gone safely under the glacier to the other side. So the others began building canoes to follow them. Finally one day the people saw them returning over the top of the glacier. They reported that the water was swift but safe. All of the families then got into their canoes and went under the glacier until they met on the other side.

"And that is how we came to this place, which the oldest ones named Lake-shaped-like-a-hip. There were so many of us that it was not possible for all to camp on the lower Stikine River, so we divided. Those who stayed in the upper camp came to be called 'Nanyaayi people' and those who went farther out became the 'Outer-sand people.'"

Marriage Plans for Kahtahah

One day Snook and his wife sat alone in the smokehouse. They had sent the whole household a few miles down the shore to picnic and to gather shau, or black mussels (called gumboots by the white traders), which clung tightly to the rocks at very low tide. Snook had not gone because the long scars on his legs made by the grizzly bear were very painful, and his wife was watching the fresh blubber in the cooking pots.

Snook's wife said, "Kahtahah will soon be a woman. It's time we think of her marriage."

Snook sat silent for a long time. At last he said, "I do not wish to think of her marriage."

"We must think of it," his wife answered. "She must have girls to bear her family name. Since the smallpox, only a few of her name are left. It is a great name."

Snook answered sadly, "She does not wish to marry so soon. I have promised her. She's only a child."

"You can see how beautiful she has become this summer. Already the white prospectors up the Stikine have looked at her with longing eyes. I sent her into the house three times last winter so the white men would not see her," his wife told him.

"I know the white men. They are bad for all of us. They bring sickness and teach us to drink liquor. They come and they go, but who knows where?" asked Snook, more in sorrow than in anger.

"We must arrange a marriage before this danger comes to her."
Snook shook his head again. "There is no young man of her
caste in our village."

"There are other villages, and her husband need not be a
young man. Young men are foolish. They have no
wealth, and they have not proved themselves," his
wife answered gently. Snook did not answer.
"I hear that a chief of the Haidas will give a
feast soon," she continued. "You will be able
to find a suitable man among them."
But Snook was firm. "Kahtahah is only a child.
There is plenty of time. I shall do nothing."
"We are growing old, and shall soon be gone.
Who will then save her from the white
man's ways? She will meet the fate
of her mother. You have spoiled the
child since she was a baby!"
His wife's voice grew high in anger.

How Kahtahah
Came to Snook's House

◆◆◆◆◆◆◆◆◆◆◆◆◆◆◆◆◆◆◆◆◆◆◆◆◆◆◆◆◆◆◆◆◆◆◆◆

That night Snook could not sleep. Though the pain in his scarred legs was heavy, his heart was heavier still. He knew his wife had spoken the truth about Kahtahah.

He remembered the first time he had seen her. A small canoe had drawn up to the beach before his Great House. In it were a man and a woman, their faces burned by the sun and the wind, their clothes stained by the rain. The woman was dressed in the curious garb that white women wear.

"It is Snook's nephew. He is returning before the others," the people called to one another.

A part of the Stikheenquan had gone down to Victoria early in the spring with canoe loads of furs to trade. Snook had sent one of his nephews with furs to be exchanged at the Hudson's Bay Company for blankets, powder for their guns and other things.

Now his nephew had returned in a small canoe with a woman companion. Snook walked down to the water's edge and looked in the canoe. In the middle was a small pile of blankets. The pile moved, and a little girl sat up then an older one. The smaller one held out her arms to Snook, speaking in English, which Snook could not understand, but he took the child into his arms and into his heart.

He turned to the mother. "I know you," he said. "You are Hoont'hut. You have come home to your own people. You belong to my wife's family. Therefore you are welcome to my house."

Their story was soon told. A number of years before, some men and women of their village had gone to Victoria to trade, but some of the women married white men

there and did not return home. Hoont'hut was one of them. She had given birth to two baby girls. When Hoont'hut was ill with the coughing sickness, she heard her husband tell another man that he thought Hoont'hut would die, so he planned to send the babies to his old home in Scotland.

To Hoont'hut this was unthinkable because a Tlingit child belongs to the mother and the mother's people, so she made her own plans. When the next party of men came from the north to trade, she found Snook's nephew and told him her story.

After the nephew finished trading for Snook, he gave the new blankets and other goods to another member of the party to take home in the large canoe and loaded one of the small, fast canoes with food. When all was ready Hoont'hut took her two small babies secretly to the canoe. They slipped silently away in the night to make the long, lonely trip back to her old home, paddling over 600 miles, sometimes across open water, in a small dugout canoe.

The Feast of Naming

The winter following the return of Hoont'hut and her children, Snook and his nephews and slaves captured many mink, marten, land otter and beaver, and even one sea otter, a rarity since the Russians and their Aleut hunters had killed so many. They traded their skins to the Hudson's Bay Company for a huge load of blankets, buttons, beads, tobacco and other white man's things. Snook did not trade for liquor, nor for molasses to make hootch. He was afraid of liquor, which put evil spirits into a man. Snook was a wise Tlingit.

A huge cache was made of the trade goods in the woods because all the presents for a big feast had once burned when a village caught fire. Since that time the Tlingits had always made their caches in the forest. No one feared a fire in a Tlingit forest. There was too much rain!

When autumn came Snook gave a week-long feast for the two little girls to make them Ahnyuddi (high caste) and to give them their names ceremonially. He gave the feast because they were relatives of his wife, although it was the Tlingit custom for the wife's brothers to give such a feast. But all the men who were

closely related to the children had died in the smallpox epidemic or had left the village.

At the top of Kahtahah's totem pole was the Raven, her mother's totem. Her frog blanket, with the design outlined in white Hudson's Bay buttons, was placed around her shoulders. Although the design would have been made of little pieces of shiny abalone shell or long white dentalium shells in the old days, Snook was proud that he could buy buttons from the white traders. Kahtahah's marten skin robe was fastened over the frog blanket. Only a chief's daughters could wear marten fur.

The two sisters were then placed on top of a huge pile of blankets. (The higher the pile of blankets, the greater the esteem in which Snook would be held by his guests.) The people danced, sang and told stories. Kahtahah could remember nothing about the feast except sitting on the blankets and looking at the jumping, whirling people below.

There were many guests from the Wolf tribe from other villages, and when they went home they took all the blankets and other things as presents. So that all the guests might have a share, some of the blankets were cut in two, but this did not lessen the value of such a present.

When the feast was over, Kahtahah and Tsoonkla were Ahnyuddi, and the stigma of a white father had been removed. Hoont'hut, however, would not allow holes to be made in the children's lower lips for a labret, a piece of bone that old-time Tlingit women wore as a sign of their high caste. Hoont'hut had learned from the white people that a labret made a woman ugly.

Snook's wife did a very unusual thing when she chose the names for the children. She gave Kahtahah a man's name, Kahkleyudt, a high name in the Teehitton tribe. So many of the men had died from smallpox that many of the high names were not held by any living person. Something about the tiny girl, some strength already apparent in her nature, made her decide on a man's name. Kahtahah found the name too hard to say with her baby tongue and promptly shortened it to Kahtahah, by which she was known ever after.

Hoont'hut died of the coughing sickness and Kahtahah forgot her English words. Sometime after, Gush, chief of the Teehitton house, a blood relative of Hoont'hut, came to Snook, wanting the children. Girls are very important to the Tlingits because the family name passes through the female line. He said that Hoont'hut's children should live in a Teehitton house since she had been born in the Teehitton family. It was not the custom for a Raven child to live in a Wolf house. The Teehitton family had lost many women in the smallpox epidemic that had swept over the village of the Stikheenquan, and they needed Hoont'hut's children to rebuild the family name.

Snook admitted the logic of the Teehitton's claim, but he had had the children too long to give them up easily. Kahtahah, especially, was very dear to him. He said that the claim should have been made when he gave the feast of adoption. He argued that though they had become his foster children, they had never ceased to belong to the Teehitton tribe and therefore could pass on the Teehitton name to their children. Many solemn councils were held that winter before the matter was finally settled. Kahtahah stayed with Snook and Tsoonkla went to live in the Teehitton house.

Visitors to the village had always noticed the fair skin and brown hair of the two children. Once a ship captain had even tried to take them away with him because he said they must be white children, but the Indians would not let them go. For many years Snook never let Kahtahah out of his sight.

As the years passed Snook came to fear the white men more and more. He saw his people die by the hundreds from measles and smallpox, and saw them grow crazy with liquor. He saw the white traders greedy and grasping in their trade with the Indians. Worst of all, he saw the young people forgetting their good Tlingit customs and copying the white man's ways. The nephews were already forgetting the respect due their uncles. And so Snook's heart was heavy as he lay that summer night thinking of what might happen to Kahtahah. He had been careful to teach her all the good Tlingit wisdom and history and the honor of her caste. He did not know what else he could do to prepare her for life.

The Death of Hoont'hut

◆◆◆◆◆◆◆◆◆◆◆◆◆◆◆◆◆◆◆◆◆◆◆◆◆◆◆◆◆◆◆◆◆◆◆◆◆◆◆

Kahtahah could remember many things connected with her real mother's death. After Snook adopted her, she was taught to call his wife by the name of mother, and her own mother became only one of the many aunts who lived in the house. Hoont'hut had lain sick for a long time on a pile of soft furs at one side of the big house near the center fire. Sometimes her body shook with terrible coughing and bloody foam came to her lips. With the indifference of childhood Kahtahah paid little attention to her suffering.

One day Snook's household was invited to a feast at another Great House. Since Snook knew that the chief had a barrel of molasses which he had made into rum, and that the feast would last until the rum was gone, Snook left Kahtahah at home in the care of a slave woman. In the night when Kahtahah was awakened by Hoont'hut's heavy breathing, Hoont'hut and Kahtahah were alone in the house. The slave, who had become frightened, had gone for help. Kahtahah threw more wood on the fire until the light blazed up and ran to Hoont'hut's side. The dying woman reached feebly for Kahtahah's hand and tried to pat it with her other hand, but she did not have the strength. The child crouched by her mother's side and held her limp hands between both of hers until they turned cold. She was still holding them when Snook and the rest of his household returned with the slave woman. Then Kahtahah crept away to the storeroom and hid, shivering, behind a box of food until Snook found her.

Hoont'hut's body was immediately taken to the Teehitton's house on the other side of the bay, and the mourning feast began. The wailing and the dancing continued for two days while the young men of the Wolf clan gathered wood for the cremation fire.

Kahtahah could remember little about those two days, but the sight of her mother's body lifted high on the pile of wood, the flames dancing around it and the young men carrying more wood to pile on the heap remained vividly in her memory.

When the ashes grew cold the people of the Wolf clan gathered them and placed them in the back of the Raven pole, which stood in front of the Teehitton House. This was the last cremation in that spot where all the Teehitton dead had been burned from time immemorial. The white people did not approve of the Indians burning their dead in this manner, so Kahtahah knew that in later years all bodies, except the shaman's, were taken to a secret place for burning, and the ashes brought back for burial at the foot of his house pole. The old people said that the bodies were burned because it made them more comfortable and their spirits would not be cold, but the bodies of the shaman were never burned.

Summer Comes to an End

All too soon the summer drew to a close. The sockeye run was followed by the pink salmon, and then by the run of large cohoe salmon. The people did not dry the pink, or humpback, salmon because its flesh was too soft, but with the cohoe, the women began cutting again on the beach where the tide would carry away the scraps and keep the camp clean. The alder wood smoke began curling through the cracks of the smokehouses.

Flocks of *touwuk* (wild geese) followed their honking leaders in long V shapes, bound for the south, and almost every day one of the young men brought in a fat *touwuk* that he had shot in the early morning. Every time a canoe went around a bend in the river a flock of mallard ducks rose straight into the air.

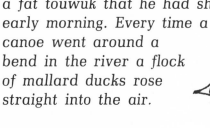

Kahtahah knew the story that explained why the mallards, or upwards-like-an-arrow birds, rose in that way. At one time the mallards flew up at a slanting angle like the black water ducks, but a mallard once struck a stick and wounded himself badly. Since that time all mallards rise straight into the air. (That is why the Tlingits call them "upward they fly.")

It had been a good summer, and the people were merry. All the berries were gathered—salmonberries, blueberries and red huckleberries. The golden cloudberries that dotted the swamps had been spread to dry in the sun and then pressed into sweet, rich cakes. The sour highbush cranberries were preserved in boxes of seal oil. The little yellow crab apples, so hard to pick because of the thorns that caught the hair and clothes, had been steamed in the pit ovens and packed in seal oil. The white long strips of the lining of hemlock bark had been steamed tender in the pit ovens and packed into cakes for winter eating. The bark cakes were softened in water to become sweet and juicy to chew following the dried salmon course.

The women tied the nicely cured skins of hair seal, deer and bear into huge bundles with red cedar bark ropes. The dried salmon were carefully wiped free of smoke and soot and packed in boxes. Their supply of food was so great that the canoes had to

make several trips back and forth to the winter village. One woman and her children went back on each trip, and Snook, his wife and Kahtahah followed in the last canoe. Some of the young men were left behind to trap winter furs, especially beaver in the many ponds a few miles back of the summer camp. Beaver skins brought a good price.

As the big Eagle canoe ran swiftly through the pass on the beginning of the down tide, Kahtahah looked back at the broad, calm salt lake. A few tall spikes of ragged fireweed were still standing, and the leaves of the highbush cranberry were turning red and yellow. The musky wild roses had dropped their pink petals and were showing their bright red seed pods. Behind the fireweed, the cranberry bushes and the roses loomed the dark green, almost black evergreen trees—hemlock, spruce and red cedar—and occasional masses of white-trunked alder trees with their yellow-green leaves.

"Summer camp is the most beautiful place in the whole world," she thought.

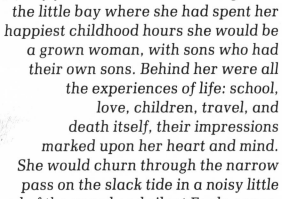

Kahtahah did not know that this would be the last time she saw the summer camp for many, many years. When she came again to the little bay where she had spent her happiest childhood hours she would be a grown woman, with sons who had their own sons. Behind her were all the experiences of life: school, love, children, travel, and death itself, their impressions marked upon her heart and mind. She would churn through the narrow pass on the slack tide in a noisy little gas boat instead of the proud and silent Eagle canoe. The long-legged cranes would lift their huge gray bodies with hoarse cries of alarm and settle at a safe distance to watch the strange visitors suspiciously. The clamor of the engine would shatter the age-old stillness of the salt lake ringed in dark cedar trees, completely out of place in that ancient setting where the Eagle canoe had floated majestically for so many summers.

The Eagle canoe itself did not make many more trips to the summer camp. Not long after, it was drawn up on the beach and left to lie exposed to the sun and rain and snow without its protective coverings. Split, faded and weather-worn, it finally attracted the attention of a man from a museum, who bought it

and shipped it many miles away to a great city, where the holes were patched and the design protected against further fading.

Many years later, Kahtahah visited her oldest son in the same great city, New York. She went to the American Museum of Natural History to show her son her old friend, the Eagle canoe. There it lay, only a wreck of its former beautiful self, no longer the proud Eagle canoe. But it brought back to Kahtahah a clear picture of the summer camp on that September afternoon long ago, and she grew suddenly homesick for the sweet, simple life on the salt lake.

Kahtahah Loses Her Painted House Front

One afternoon most of the children of the Stikheenquan were playing on the beach. The boys were skipping stones on the water when suddenly one slipped from a boy's hand and struck a playmate on the temple. The boy fell to the sand, blood flowing from the jagged cut.

Kahtahah pulled up some dry grass and pressed it against the cut while Tsoonkla ran for help. It seemed only an instant before the children were surrounded by all the grown people of the village. Kahtahah was jerked violently away by the boy's mother, who loudly demanded to know who had struck her son. She herself made no effort to stop the flow of blood, but continued such a loud barrage of talking that she would have been unable to hear any answer given. Kahtahah slipped down beside the boy again and pressed the grass back into place.

The boy who had thrown the stone stood alone, white-faced and trembling. He well understood his danger, for if the boy should die, his own life would be demanded in exchange. The fact that it was an accident made no difference.

As soon as the screaming woman realized who had hurt her son she rushed at him and would have scratched his eyes out if his uncle had not snatched him away. She then rushed at the boy's mother and the two women stood face to face, both violently shrieking at each other. Meanwhile the injured boy sat up. It was plain that he was not badly hurt, but the situation was still serious.

Leaving the women to scream at each other, the head chiefs of all the houses of the village met in council. Since the boy was not killed, according to custom peace could be made by the payment of blankets to the injured family. Otherwise the boy who had thrown the stone must become the slave of the injured boy's family until he was redeemed. The council met to decide what number of blankets would be satisfactory according to the caste of the families concerned. These were very serious matters and took a long time to talk over, and the solemn council was still meeting long after the injured boy was back playing on the beach with the others. The council decided that 30 blankets would satisfy his family since the injured boy's caste was not very high. The price could have been as high as 100 blankets.

Snook brought the news back to his house late that night.

"But how can they ever pay even 30 blankets?" Kahtahah cried.

"I don't think they can pay more than 10 blankets. They are not rich. Yet 30 blankets is a fair price," he answered soberly.

"Will the poor boy then be a slave to that terrible woman?" Kahtahah asked. "I am sorry for him."

"That woman has never had slaves," Snook's wife said. "She doesn't know how to deal with slaves. I'm sorry for the boy, too."

Snook was not at all surprised when the boy's uncles came to his house the next morning. They begged Snook to loan them the blankets to make the required payment and promised to give the boy to Snook as security until they could repay the blankets. They belonged to the Wolf clan, so it was fitting that they should turn to the Nanyaayi tribe for help. People knew that Snook was rich.

He had many blankets stored away in a cache for some purpose, probably a great feast. Only Snook himself knew that he was planning to bring in a Haida painter to paint a story over the front of his house, which would make Snook's name high indeed because no one in the Stikine village had a painted house front. When the house was ready he would give a feast.

Snook spoke roughly to the uncles, "Have you ever earned 30 blankets in your whole lives, all of you together? I don't believe you could ever repay me."

"Then the boy will be your slave forever," they answered.

"I don't need more slaves," Snook replied. "He would be just one more mouth to feed. I'll be dead before he is old enough to earn his food. No, no, I have other plans for my blankets. Go to someone who needs slaves more than I do."

After the men had gone, Kahtahah begged for the boy. "He is small, father, to belong to that woman. I was sure she was going to scratch his eyes out yesterday. He looked so scared, but he did not run. It is not much for you to pay 30 blankets."

"You know they will never earn the blankets to pay me back," Snook answered.

"Oh, yes, I know that." Then Kahtahah looked soberly at her foster father. "Why are you saving blankets, father?" she asked. Snook slowly and thoughtfully filled his pipe with tobacco and smoked a while before he answered her. Then he began, "Have you ever been told about the house in which your grandmother, Hoont'hut's mother, was born? When her mother went from the Tongass people to marry the Haida chief she took with her many slaves and boxes full of blankets and coppers and other treasures. That house was built especially for her and a big feast was given in her honor.

"I heard my uncle tell the story of the feast. He was proud to be a guest because before that, the mother of the Tongass princess had come from his own people among the Stikheenquan. The circle is back here again, complete with you. It is my purpose to have the same story painted on the front of the house that will be yours. I am saving blankets for that.

"That is a story of your own family and it is your right to have such a story painted on your own house," Snook finished.

"But father," Kahtahah said slowly, "I do not much care about such a house. I'm happy here with you. If that is the only reason you do not give the men the blankets, I would feel unhappy every time I looked at that poor boy."

"Such a house front would make your name higher than any in the village of the Stikine," Snook said.

Kahtahah's head went up proudly.

"My name is high already. I have a man's name. I remember what the shaman said when I was sick. I would rather you gave the blankets for the boy."

Snook looked at his wife. She answered his unspoken question. "I, too, would be sorry to see any child a slave to that woman."

Snook laid aside his pipe. "It is decided. Send for the boy's uncles."

When the men arrived Snook had already counted out the 30 big Hudson's Bay blankets. In exchange he received the boy as a slave until his family could redeem him. That day never came, as Snook expected.

A Haida Chief Gives a Feast

When the September rains had blown away, a messenger came to the winter village of the Stikheenquan carrying an invitation from Skowl, a great chief of the Haidas, to all the Wolf families, for a feast in a month's time. Invitations had also been sent to the Tsimshian country to the south. Everyone knew that this was to be a great feast, and the canoe of the chief's messenger, his grandson, was sent away loaded with presents. These gifts showed the respect the Stikine people had for the Haida chief.

At the appointed time, Snook's largest canoe and others from the other Wolf houses left the village of the Stikheenquan for a month of merrymaking in the Haida village. Snook carried two red camphor wood chests filled with dancing costumes and Chilkat blankets.

Snook was a famous dancer. He knew all the old ceremonial dances and the songs that went with them. In spite of his age he would put on the family hat with the Eagle crest to lead the dancing for his side. On the top of the hat was a round basket filled with swan's down which fluttered around like snow as he danced. In the eagle's beak were locks of hair from the four slaves that were killed at the feast when the hat was dedicated in very olden times. Snook's dancing stick was decorated with hair from eight enemies he had killed in battle in his youth.

The trip was very different from that to the summer camp. The days had grown so short that the canoes started long before daylight. The water was smoothest then on the wide mouth of the Stikine with its white glacial water. The young men paddled in relays because no stops were made, even at night. The whole trip was made under leaden skies. If the weather had been fair they would have stopped at several places to rest and to practice their dances and songs.

The Haida village was packed with many guests. Three different languages were spoken—Tlingit, Haida and Tsimshian. There were some, however, in each group who could speak all three tongues. Kahtahah had never seen so many totem poles; the village looked like a forest of gaily painted poles, and around the point was another forest of grave totems where the Haidas burned their dead.

Chief Skowl's house was the largest in the village. In front of the house stood two totem poles carved exactly alike. At the top of each was the raven, the chief's clan. The raven was placed high above the other figures on the poles to show the great dignity of the family. Below it was another raven with the moon in his mouth (once the raven stole the moon from its keeper and gave it to the earth people), and below that were the many wives of the raven. The lowest figure was the whale. Kahtahah knew that story:

One day when Raven was wandering around near the mouth of the Alsek River he saw a large whale blowing its misty breath into the air far out to sea. Raven, who was always hungry, was especially fond of whale blubber, so he was very eager to catch *this fine sea animal. Since he had neither hook nor line, he sat down on the beach to figure out how he could bring it ashore.*

Raven noticed that when the whale came to the surface its mouth was wide open, so Raven flew out to the whale with his fire bag of flint, stone and tinder. The next time it opened its mouth Raven flew in and sat down in the far corner of its stomach, where he built a fire. When the whale swallowed small fish such as trout and herring, Raven caught them and cooked them for himself. Becoming greedy, he cut out the whale's heart and cooked and ate it. The whale died then, and Raven could feel the whale no longer swimming, but drifting about from place to place.

He began singing a song: "Let the whale go ashore. Let the whale go ashore upon a sandy beach," and before long he heard the sound of waves breaking on the shore and felt the whale rolling up on the beach.

So he sang again, "Let the one who wants to be high caste like me cut the whale open and let me out; then he will be as high as I am!"

He sang on until he heard the voices of young people near him. They were surprised to hear the strange sounds coming from the whale that had been washed ashore and began cutting into it. All of the villagers rushed down to help, and as soon as the opening around the blowhole was large enough, out flew Raven, crying "Klon-ee! Klon-ee!"

Raven stayed up in the woods a long time, cleaning the grease and smell of the whale from his feathers. Meanwhile, the people were overjoyed to possess such a valuable prize, although they were puzzled by the strange singing in the whale and startled by the strange bird that had burst forth. They set to work at once to try out the blubber and filled many boxes with whale grease.

At last Raven appeared in the form of a man. He acted surprised and asked the people how they had caught the whale. They told him it had washed up on the beach right where they could get it easily, so they were making oil from it. Said Raven, "Did you hear a strange sound inside the whale when it first came ashore?"

"Yes!" the people answered. "There was a strange sound like singing, and something flew out calling 'Klon-ee! Klon-ee!'"

Raven then told them that long ago the same thing had happened in his country, and all the people who had eaten the grease had died. He said, "It brings bad luck to hear singing inside a whale. You people must leave these boxes right away. Don't eat any of the whale!"

The people were so badly frightened that they ran away at once, leaving the grease boxes lying on the beach, and Raven sat down and ate all the grease he wanted. That was the kind of trick that the raven liked to play.

Chief Skowl's new pole that was to be dedicated at this feast was also in front of his house. It was being erected in honor of his daughter, to make her children Ahnyuddi. Since she had married a white man the American eagle was carved at the top of her pole.

Near Chief Sunny Heart's house stood the fog woman pole. A carver had taken three years to make the pole—the most beautiful one Kahtahah had ever seen—with only an adz made from a steel file, sharpened and fastened to a crooked branch of wood.

At the top of the pole was the fog woman who was married to the sun. Below were her two children, the salmon and the green leaves that come in the spring, and below that, the wolf, which was Chief Sunny Heart's clan. Next came many figures that represented the guests at the great feast given for the erection of the pole.

For a whole month Chief Skowl entertained his guests with ceremonial feasting, dancing and storytelling. All the villages competed in the dances, songs and stories. For their first dance the Stikheenquan danced a Tsimshian dance: Many, many years before, a large war party of Tsimshians had been defeated by the Stikines near the mouth of the Stikine River, and many Tsimshian chiefs had been captured. After the Stikine people feasted them for several days, they put the Tsimshian chiefs in canoes and sent them home unharmed. This gave the Stikheenquan chiefs the right to take the names of the Tsimshian chiefs and to dance the Tsimshian dance.

All the dancers were closely watched as they danced the old dances and sang the old songs, for if they made a mistake it was a disgrace. A mistake in the old ceremonial songs and dances brought shame to their whole village. The other guests called insults at them and made great sport of them.

Of many dances that Snook had the right to dance was the bear dance. With advancing age, he had given the right to this dance to a nephew, the son of his oldest sister, who would succeed him as chief of his house. This young man appeared before the people walking like a bear. He acted out the story of Snook's famous fight with the grizzly bear, and also danced the dance that told the story of the bear's climbing the mountain to escape the great flood that happened long before any man's memory. He wore a bear skin with its claws sheathed in copper.

Several men were present whose business was to make up new songs and dances. They were always great clowns who amused everybody, and when one rose to speak or sing the people laughed before he uttered a word.

How the Bear Clan Obtained the Eagle for Its Totem

Many hours were passed in telling stories. The people of the Wolf clan would make speeches about how wise, strong and full of good luck their emblem, the Eagle, was. One of the great favorites of the Tsimshian men was how the chief of the Bear family, which belongs to the Wolf clan, obtained the right to use the Eagle for its crest. Many totem poles, called "Good Luck Totems," have been carved to tell this story.

Once a great chief of the Bear family lived with his four brothers-in-law and an only son in a large town near a sand bar on the Nass River. The boy liked to sit on top of his father's house and make arrows, which needed eagle feathers to fly straight.

When summer came and the rivers were filled with humpback salmon, the people went fishing every day and dried many thousands of fish for winter use. Even the little boy caught many humpback salmon, which he always unloaded on the sand bar in front of the village. But every morning during the whole summer the eagles gathered and ate all his catch. When the eagles grew

fat with so much food they dropped their feathers on the sand bar, and the little boy sent his slave to gather them. The chief's little son fed the eagles deliberately because he wanted their feathers for his many arrows.

When winter came and food grew scarce, the father remembered that his son had fed his fish to the eagles all summer long. He said to the boy's uncles, "I don't want any of you to take pity on my son when he comes to ask for food. Remember how he fed the eagles during the salmon run. Let the eagles feed him now!" The uncles promised.

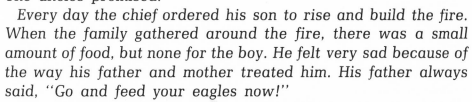

Every day the chief ordered his son to rise and build the fire. When the family gathered around the fire, there was a small amount of food, but none for the boy. He felt very sad because of the way his father and mother treated him. His father always said, "Go and feed your eagles now!"

One day he went to the house of his oldest uncle, who told his wife to spread a mat by the fire and bring him food. She roasted a piece of dried salmon on the fire, put it in a dish and set it before the boy. As he reached out his hand to take the fish his uncle rose quickly and took it away, and said, "Go and ask the eagles that you fed last summer to feed you now!" Then he and his wife ate the fish. The boy was very much ashamed of the way his uncle treated him.

The next day he went to the second uncle's house, where the same thing happened. First, food was placed before him, and then his uncle took it away and ate it himself. He also told his nephew to ask the eagles for food. The boy went sadly away.

The following morning he went to the third uncle's house, where his uncle's wife roasted a dried salmon. But before he could touch it his uncle said, "Oh, this is the boy who feeds the eagles!" and took it away. The boy cried all night.

On the fourth morning he went to his youngest uncle, who said, "I've heard what my bad brothers have done to you. Your father asked all of us to do this, but I don't wish to treat you that way." So he told his wife to roast some salmon and they fed their nephew well. He went home happy.

Early the next morning the chief said, "We must look for a place with more food," and sent his slave to tell the people to get ready to move. When they left the next day, the chief would not take his son with him, but the youngest uncle's wife left him a dried salmon and a small box of eulachon oil. His little slave boy stayed with him.

After the people left, the little son made himself a small house from some old boards and cedar bark and sat down beside it with his arrows. The tide was low and an eagle stood on the sand bar screaming. The boy told his slave to go down to the beach to see why it was screaming.

When the slave went to the sand bar, the eagle flew away. But on the spot where the eagle had stood lay a bright, silver trout. The slave carried it up to his master, and they roasted it for that day's food.

The next day another eagle left a bullhead in its place, and for several days thereafter the eagles gave them bullheads and trout. But one day they heard the sound of many eagles and found a silver salmon, which they dried. Every morning for a while they found a silver salmon, and before long, the boy's house was full of dried salmon.

Then the eagles began to leave large halibuts on the sand bar, so the boy and his slave built another house, which they filled with dried halibut.

The eagles next brought them a house full of seal meat, then a house full of sea lion meat, and finally, they brought whales, which they tied to the beach with cedar bark rope.

Meanwhile, the people who had gone farther up the Nass River could find no food, not even eulachon, and the people began to die of starvation.

Back in their old village the chief's son and his slave had filled all the houses with dried fish, meat and whale blubber. He thought about his youngest uncle who had been kind to him and was afraid that he had no food. Calling a sea gull to him, he said, "Let me take your skin for a while," whereupon the sea gull lent him his skin. The boy flew up the river with a piece of roasted seal meat in his mouth until he found the people, who were out in canoes trying to catch eulachon, but there were none in the river. The chief's son flew around until he found a slave woman who belonged to his father and dropped the seal meat in her lap. She took the meat, but kept quiet about it until she reached home. She fed the bit of seal meat to her little girl, but she was so hungry that she choked on it and could not get her breath. Everybody was frightened, and the chief's wife put her finger down the child's throat and pulled it out.

When she saw that it was food, she called her husband. The chief asked the slave where she got the meat, and she said that a gull had dropped it in her lap while she was out fishing.

"Which way did the gull fly?" the chief asked, and the woman answered, "Straight back down the river."

The chief called all his wise men to ask their advice, and they told him they thought that his son was still alive. The chief sent a canoe back to their old village to see what had happened. The messengers were so weak from hunger that they could hardly paddle, and they merely floated down the river with the current for most of the journey. As they came near the sand bar they saw that the water was covered with grease, and that there were four large whales, many bones lying about, and houses filled with food. They were overcome with wonder and surprise.

The chief's son stood on the beach to meet them, but would not let them land. They begged for mercy because they were weak from hunger, so he fed them salmon, seal meat and blubber for two whole days. Then he sent them back with the admonition, "Don't tell my father that I am alive and well. Tell him I died long ago, but secretly get word to my youngest uncle that I have food for him. I will give him a whole whale; the others must buy their food from me."

They paddled upstream as quickly as they could and told everything. They told the chief that his son was still alive, and that the houses were filled to overflowing with dried salmon, trout, halibut, seal and sea lion meat; that there were four large whales lying on the beach, and boxes of grease were everywhere. They said that all of it belonged to the boy. He did not want to see his father or mother and would give food only to his youngest uncle. The rest had to buy it. No one slept that night, but quickly packed their things to return to their village the next morning. The chief said, "We will ask my son to have pity on us."

The oldest uncle had dressed his two daughters in their best clothes to offer them in marriage to his nephew. As they neared the village they saw that the water was covered with grease. They were so hungry that they dipped their fingers and licked the grease from them. When the chief's son saw them coming he called, "Do not come ashore. I don't want you. If you come I will shoot you with my arrows. Go away and leave me to starve."

But the people begged for food. The boy asked, "Where is my youngest uncle?"

He would not allow them to land until his youngest uncle had come ashore. He gave him the largest whale and received his uncle's daughter for his wife in return. Then the boy called to the people to come nearer. When he saw how they caught the grease that was floating on the water, he was ashamed, and forgetting how they had left him to starve, gave food to everybody.

Next morning they came to buy food from him, bringing skins, slaves, canoes, abalone shells, copper shields and many kinds of rich furs like marten and sea otter. He became richer than all the other chiefs, and when he married his youngest uncle's daughter he gave a great feast. He gave presents of elk skins and dancing blankets, horn spoons and abalone shells, copper shields and necklaces of killer whale teeth. His name became greater than that of any other Tsimshian chief.

All this had happened because the eagles brought him good luck, and ever since, his family has always claimed the Eagle as their emblem, or totem.

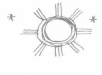

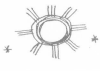

How Raven Brought Daylight to Mankind

◆◆◆◆◆◆◆◆◆◆◆◆◆◆◆◆◆◆◆◆◆◆◆◆◆◆◆◆◆◆◆◆◆◆◆◆◆◆◆

After the Tsimshian visitor had finished the eagle story, Snook rose to tell how Raven brought daylight to the world. All the people of the Wolf clan liked to tell how clever and tricky Raven was. He was a wicked fellow but had given the Indians many useful things—the sun, the moon, the stars, fire—and even before that, had scattered salmon and trout eggs over the rivers so that all the streams came to be filled with fish.

All this had happened before the beginning of things-as-they-are, when the whole earth lay in darkness. The chief of the over-sky people owned all the daylight as well as the moon and the stars, which he kept hanging in bundles and boxes high on the walls of his house. Once a year he allowed a few rays to escape from the great round box in which he kept the sun, so that the over-sky people could have light, but only a few dim rays came through the hole-in-the-sky to the dark earth. Raven grieved because his people had no light and decided to steal the daylight from the over-sky chief, who was called Raven-who-lived-at-the-head-of-the-Nass-River. First he put on his raven blanket and flew and flew into the sky until he found the hole-in-the-sky and slipped through into the over-sky country.

The clever bird knew that the sun, the moon and the stars were kept in boxes hanging on the walls of the chief's house, and that in some way he had to get inside the room to reach them. He took off his raven blanket, and leaving it by the hole-in-the-sky, sought out the chief's house.

He began to observe the chief's daughter very carefully and learned that every day she drank from the spring behind her home. So Raven changed himself into a hemlock needle and floated on the water. The next time the princess drank from the spring she swallowed the hemlock needle, which was really Raven, so that he might be born into the chief's family. After a while a child—Raven—was born to the princess. Raven began to grow rapidly in the home of the over-sky chief, with the daylight and the moon and the stars hanging in boxes high on the walls. He was soon too large for his cradle swing. His grandfather was filled with pride and joy because no other chief had ever had so fine and strong a grandson. So mighty was the baby Raven that the ground shook when he beat the floor in his play.

One day Raven began to cry and wouldn't stop. His mother and grandmother tried to comfort him, but they could find nothing to please him. The chief came, but Raven cried harder than ever. The chief called a slave to carry the child around to quiet him, but still Raven cried and called for something.

"What is he saying?" asked his mother.

"What is he saying?" echoed his grandmother.

The chief called in the wise ones of the over-sky country to tell him what the child was crying for. To some it seemed as if the child was crying, "Caw! Caw!" but one old man said it was "Quook, quook!" and that he was crying for the box on the wall.

The chief ordered a slave to take down the box containing the moon. He placed it near the fire where the child could reach it. Raven stopped crying at once and began to laugh. "Ha, ha!" he said, but to some it sounded like "Caw, caw!"

Raven was happy. He reached for the box, but it slipped through his fingers when he touched it. It flew up through the smoke hole into the sky, where it hangs to this day, spreading its silver light.

Again Raven burst into tears, and his roars of anger echoed through the room. He pointed to the bundles on the wall and wept continually. At last his grandfather said, "Give my grandchild what he is crying for. Give him the bag of stars at the end."

So Raven stopped crying and played with the bag of stars, rolling it around the room back of the people, but suddenly he let it go up through the smoke hole. It went straight to the sky to join the moon. The stars fell out and arranged themselves as you see them today.

Raven again roared with anger and pointed to the walls of his grandfather's house. Because his grandfather thought he might die, he ordered the great round box of daylight to be untied and given to him. Raven's eyes rolled around and turned different colors in his joy at receiving the coveted box. All day he rolled it around the room, and all night he slept with it beside his mat.

Some in the over-sky country were fearful because a child, even the chief's grandson, was playing with so precious a possession as the box of daylight. But no one dared complain to the chief, who would become very angry and roar, "Be silent, or I will pull out your tongue like the cormorant's was pulled out."

For four days the child Raven played with the box. Some times he pounded it with all his might and shouted, "Quook, quook!" His voice had grown so loud that even his old grandmother said, "How like a raven the child sounds!"

Toward evening of the fourth day Raven quietly rolled the box near the door. He knew that the right time had come because no one was watching him—the chief was dreaming by the fire and the women were busy with their duties. Lifting the great round

box of daylight to his shoulders, Raven ran out the door and turned toward the hole-in-the-sky. But outside the door stood one who had been apprehensive about the child. When he saw Raven running away he called loudly, "Look, look! The prince is running away with the box!" Others, hearing him, repeated the cry.

All of the over-sky people began to run after Raven, filling the over-sky with the noise of their crying and running. The lid of the box loosened as Raven ran, and a little daylight spilled out onto the ground. Because of the leaking daylight streaming behind him, the over-sky people had no trouble following Raven's trail through the forests and along the valleys. At last he came to the hole-in-the-sky, where he wrapped his raven blanket tightly around him so that all the light was hidden. With a last taunting, "Caw, caw!" he slipped quietly through the hole-in-the-sky to his own earth. The over-sky people knew that they had lost him and went sadly back to their homes without the precious box of daylight.

The raven blanket, acting like wings, carried Raven back to his own country on the Nass River. As he flew through the air he passed through the smoke of many villages that men now call clouds. At each cloud village someone handed him a lighted torch, and so fast did Raven fly that the flame of the torch streamed far behind him and burned out like a shooting star.

Earth was very dark. Raven walked down the river until he heard people talking. The Frog people were out in their canoes catching eulachon in their bag nets. Raven called to them in the dark for some fresh water. The water of all the earth was brackish; the only fresh water fell from the skies, but Raven had become fond of fresh water in the land of the over-sky people. So he said to the Frog people, "I am thirsty. Give me some fresh water."

The Frog people immediately set up a-crying and a-croaking, "Kronk, kronk! Give a stranger our water, our precious water? Never!"

Then Raven called, "I'm hungry. Give me some fresh eulachon."

The frogs laughed and croaked at him again, "Kronk, kronk! Give a stranger our fresh eulachon, the first we have caught? Never!"

Raven begged of the Frog people a last time: "I am cold. Build me a warm fire." But as before, the frogs refused, croaking, "Kronk, kronk! Give a stranger our torch of burning fire that fell from the stars? Never!"

Then Raven cried, throwing back his dark blanket, "I am Raven, and I hold in my hands the great round box of daylight that belonged only to Nass-sha-kee-yalth, the Raven who sits above the Nass head," but the frogs only retorted, "Kronk, kronk! What boasting is this? Kronk, kronk!"

Again Raven called, "I am the grandson of the over-sky chief, and I have brought the daylight from the over-sky land. The frogs shouted, "Kronk, kronk! Liar! Kronk, kronk!"

As Raven threw the great round box of daylight to the ground it burst open, and with a roar like crashing thunder, daylight rushed out and filled the earth. Its force was so great that the north wind began to blow. It blew the canoes of the Frog people down the river and far out to sea to a large island where the Frog people tried to climb to escape the north wind, but froze fast to the rocks and became part of the stones. This was their punishment for having laughed at Raven, and there they are to this day.

All of the rest of the earth's inhabitants had gathered out on the river to fish in eight canoes. When the box of daylight burst with such a roar and light flooded the earth, all were greatly frightened and tried to escape. Those who ran into the water turned into seals or porpoises, and those who ran into the woods became marten, mink and other land animals. That is how Raven created the different kinds of animals.

Six Canoes Full of Soapberries

O**n** *the next to the last day of Chief Skowl's festivities there was a soapberry contest between each village's crew of young men. They scrubbed their arms to the shoulders and cleaned small canoes carefully with sand so that no oil spots were left. Dried soapberries were then placed in each canoe with plenty*

of water. At a signal each canoe team began to beat the berries to a foam with their arms, each clan cheering for its own canoe with great noise and excitement. One of the villages from the Nass River won the contest.

When the canoes were full of foaming soapberries, Chief Skowl added some of the white man's sugar, a great treat, and the soapberries were ready to be eaten. Each person filled his biggest horn spoon with the berries. Like everyone else, Kahtahah knew how to get the best flavor from the soapberries. Filling her mouth full, she clacked her tongue against the roof of her mouth until all the sweet foam had run down her throat. Dozens of clacking tongues made a funny sound.

At the last dance each group of guests vied to see which knew the most songs. If a song leader broke down or left out part of a song it was counted against his side. Since Kahtahah knew all the songs and could sing like a bird, she was trusted to sing with the grown people in the contest. Some of the very small boys were dressed in little Chilkat blankets and danced with their uncles. Kahtahah was very proud when the Stikheenquan won. During their last song, everyone threw them presents—pieces of copper and iron, white man's money, tobacco, and even blankets.

When Chief Skowl's food and presents were gone the people left for home. Snook's canoe was overloaded with gifts. It was said that Skowl had spent $6,000 at this feast. He was no longer a rich man, but his name was high and greatly honored. That was the purpose of the feast.

Kahtahah's Frog Blanket

◆◆

At Chief Skowl's feast Kahtahah had noticed a young Haida girl wearing a frog blanket very much like the ones that belonged to her and her sister. She had wondered about it at the time because she had been taught that no other people but the Kiksuddi tribe and the Teehitton branch that had split from them had a right to the frog emblem, but everyone had been so busy then that she could not ask questions. On the trip home she asked Snook how a Haida girl could wear a frog blanket. Snook told her again the long story of how her great-great-grandmother had been given in marriage to a very rich Tongass chief.

They had two children, a boy and a girl, who in turn was married to a Haida chief. She took with her to Haida country a rich dowry of many slaves, copper pieces and blankets, including her frog blanket. The Haida chief built a fine new home to honor his Tlingit wife. Over the entire front he had painted and carved the following story of his family.

Once a chief's daughter had made fun of the spirits that lived in water-things. (He painted her face just below the heavy beams of the roof.) As her punishment, the Gunakadate (the spirit of the water) captured her and carried her away to a lonely island. (He painted Gunakadate just over the doorway: two big eyes and a mouth, and ears reaching up on each side of the chief's daughter to show that the Gunakadate had heard her unkind words.) The girl's people were alarmed at her disappearance and consulted the shaman of her tribe. The shaman told them where the girl was hidden, and the chief sent two wolves out to get her. (He had painted the wolves in the upper corners of the house front. In the lower corners he had painted the spirits of the water-things, with *fingers next to the door. These fingers were continually reaching out to seize the people who did not respect their power.)*

The Haida chief and his wife lived in the house for many years and grew richer and richer. His wife had so many slaves to wait on her that she never lifted her hand to do any work, nor did she have to care for her own children. But then her husband died, and according to custom, she married her husband's nephew. By this marriage she continued to enjoy all her comforts. But it didn't work out, and with her youngest daughter and only the frog blanket, she returned penniless to her own relatives among the Stikheenquan. The youngest daughter was Kahtahah's own grandmother, and it was this house front that Snook had planned to have made for Kahtahah.

The Haida girl who wore the frog blanket at the dance apparently belonged to the family of one of the older children who had stayed and married in the Haida country.

"How did our family first get the right to wear the Frog crest?" was Kahtahah's next question.

Snook then told her the story of how all the Kiksuddi clansmen came to claim the Frog.

This took place at the time the people lived in a place called Town-of-the-frogs because of the many frogs in the marshes nearby. One day a young man kicked over on its back a frog that

was in his path, and he immediately fell senseless to the ground. The people thought he was dead and carried his body into the house and began to mourn for him. He lay there a long time as if dead, the women wailing around him.

Suddenly the young man stood up and began to talk when his spirit, which the Frog people had taken to the house of the frogs, was restored to him. "They captured me," he said, "because of the frog that I kicked from my path, and tied me to the house post of the chief. Some wanted to kill me immediately, and some wanted to starve me, but most of them wanted to wait until their chief came home. At last their chief, Frightful Face, came in and they said to him, 'We have captured a man of the people who threw over one of our women. What shall we do with him?'

"'Untie him,' he said, and they obeyed. Then he spoke to me.

"'Do you think it right to treat a woman of your own clan so badly? Don't you know that we belong to the same clan, that you are Kiksuddi, and that we are Kiksuddi? You have brought shame, and have disgraced yourself as well as us by being cruel. If it were not that we are of the same clan we would punish you severely. As it is, you may go back to your people.'"

After the Kiksuddi people listened to the young man talk, they claimed the frog as their crest because the Frog chief himself said he was Kiksuddi.

Many years after that, there was a fight between the old and young women. The young women were defeated and moved out. They needed shelter in this rainy country, so the men made a cedar bark house (Teehit); hence the name Teehitton. They still

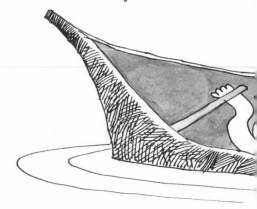

shared the Frog crest with the Kiksuddi. Only the Kiksuddi and the people who came from them use the Frog.

"But," Snook continued, "the Kiksuddi of Sitka have made local story of how they came to claim the frog for their crest:

A man and his wife were out hunting in their canoe. To get home they had to cross a large bay, but fog, so thick they could not even see the water around them, rolled in from the ocean and covered them. They stopped paddling and let their canoe drift. After a while they heard a roaring so loud that they could hear the echo roll back from the mountains around the bay. They heard singing, and words repeated in a powerful voice: "We've picked up a man; you've picked up a man," and "We've captured a man; you've captured a man."

After they had learned the song, the man and his wife began singing it with the voice. The fog lifted a little so they could see the water. The voice seemed to be coming nearer so they stopped singing and listened and looked all around. They finally saw that the powerful voice came from a very small frog, which they followed for quite a while. The man said, "This frog is going to be mine. I am going to claim it," but his wife answered, "No, I heard it first. It will be mine. I am going to claim it."

They argued for some time, but the man finally let his wife have it. When they paddled alongside the frog, she picked it up, and taking it home, treated it just like a baby. Later she carried it to the woods and left it beside the lake. All the Kiksuddi of Sitka are descended from that woman and that is why they claim the frog as their crest.

How the Cormorant Lost His Tongue

◆◆◆◆◆◆◆◆◆◆◆◆◆◆◆◆◆◆◆◆◆◆◆◆◆◆◆◆◆

Kahtahah asked one more question on the trip
home from the Haida village. "When you were telling the raven
story, father, you made the over-sky chief tell his wise men he
would pull out their tongues like the cormorant's. I don't know
that story."

Snook told her the story of how the cormorant lost his tongue.

"It happened just after the raven had tricked the sea gull out of
the herring. While Raven was flying away with the herring in his
beak he saw a village beneath him. He landed near the village and
rubbed the shiny scales of the herring all over his body before he
swallowed it. He walked into the village and acted as if he were
full of food. Raven rubbed his stomach and said to the people who

gathered about him, "My goodness, but there are lots of herring just on the other side of that far point!" When they heard what Raven had to say, they all rushed away to find the herring, because it was time for the herring run and they did not have any.

Raven now took his time. First he stole a big canoe and filled it with everything he wanted. Then he took two young men for slaves. One was Cormorant, the black diver duck that sits on the rocks, and the other was Loon, who never flies except in the springtime. The people know when the herring have come because he then calls with his one lone cry.

Loon and Cormorant paddled Raven in the big canoe until they came to another town where there was plenty of halibut. Raven asked different people for enough halibut for himself and his servants, but they only answered, "Why don't you get your own halibut? There are plenty of them right in front of the town." Finally Raven became ashamed and with his servant Cormorant went fishing for halibut.

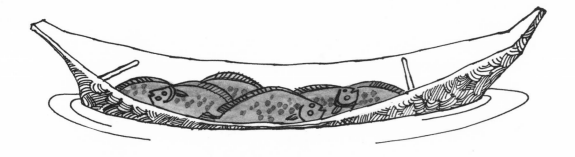

Cormorant had filled the canoe with halibut in a very short time, and they started back to the village. Now Raven had bragged so much about his skill as a fisherman that he knew he would be disgraced if the people learned that Cormorant had caught all the fish, so he began to scheme how they would not learn. He said to his servant, "My friend, what do you have on your tongue? Stick out your tongue so I can take a look."

Cormorant obeyed him and Raven seized his tongue and pulled it out. Then Raven said, "Let me hear you talk."

Cormorant tried to talk but all he could say was, "Walla-walla-walla-walla."

Raven said, "That is fine. You talk much better now than you used to." Raven felt satisfied.

When they got ashore with their halibut, the people were surprised. Raven got out of the canoe and swaggered about on the beach while his servant fastened the canoe. As Raven lifted each halibut from the canoe he began to tell the people how he had caught them. At the same time Cormorant was doing his best to tell the people that it was he who had caught all the halibut. He thought he was talking plainly, but all he said was "Walla-walla-walla-walla" and so the people paid no attention to him. Finally when Raven came to the last halibut in the canoe, the great big one that had worked its way to the very bottom of the canoe, Cormorant was frantic with anger, and jumped about, pointing and jabbing at the people, saying, "Walla-walla-walla-walla!"

Raven stopped his story and said, "See my servant? He is trying to tell you what a hard time we had to get this one into the canoe. I nearly lost my life."

Raven strutted about the town while people pointed him out to the children as a great fisherman, but the cormorant to this day sits on low rocks near the ocean, almost as silent as the rocks themselves. He has never had a tongue since the day Raven pulled it out, and once in a while, perhaps remembering the time when he could talk with people, he says, "Walla-walla-walla-walla."

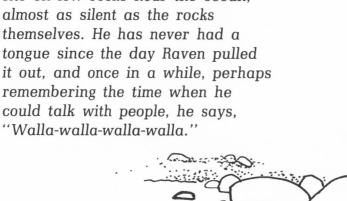

The Changing Times

◆◆◆◆◆◆◆◆◆◆◆◆◆◆◆◆◆◆◆◆◆◆◆◆◆◆◆◆◆◆◆◆◆◆◆◆◆◆◆

That winter there was trouble in the village of the Stikheenquan. Before the ice had formed some white men with gold in their pouches came down the Stikine River and built cabins at the edge of the Indian village. They took some Indian girls to live in their cabins, but did not ask for them in an honorable manner. When one man tried to talk to Kahtahah, Snook was very angry. He wanted to kill the white man, but he felt the power of the changing times.

The head chiefs of the 10 great houses of the village held many solemn councils around the center fires, but they could do nothing but talk. Over on the edge of the ocean, at Sitka, where the Russians had built their stockade, the "Boston men" now had gunboats and soldiers. No one knew when a gunboat might come to the Stikine village, and whenever the gunboat sailed up, soldiers with guns came ashore.

The captain of the gunboat called the chiefs together and said that wrongdoers had to be turned over to him for punishment. He said that the Boston men had now bought the country from the Russians, and that the chiefs of the Great Houses should no longer determine the punishment for their own households. The Indians no longer dared to demand a life for a life from those who had insulted them. Only the captain of the gunboat had the power to punish, and all the people had to obey the white man's laws, or they would be punished. Whenever the captain sailed away he had one of his big guns fired "in their honor," he said, but they knew it was a warning for them to obey.

Snook did not know what to do. He respected the captain of the gunboat and feared the power of his soldiers, but the white men living at the edge of the village were not like the captain of the gunboat. Snook wished that he still had the strength and fire of his youthful days.

One afternoon in December, just before the early dark, Kahtahah and Tsoonkla were playing across the bay outside the Teehitton house. On the ground snow lay about a foot deep with a hard crust on top. The girls were amusing themselves by stamping through the hard crust in a sort of follow-the-leader game.

Through the gray dusk they saw a small canoe draw up to the beach, and a man and a woman came to them over the white snow.

"Which house is the Great Raven House?" the man asked.

"Where the tall Raven pole is," Tsoonkla answered. "This is also a Raven house where the Teehitton live, and over there is the Kiksuddi house. You will be welcome there also."

Both the man and the woman seemed very cold and tired. They looked longingly at the nearby Teehitton house, but turned and trudged through the snow to the Great Raven House.

"They have come on a long journey," Kahtahah said. "It is hard to travel in bad weather. See how tired the woman is! She can hardly walk." They watched the strangers until they reached the Great Raven House, and then went on with their game.

Later in the evening the chief of one of the smaller Raven houses came to see Snook. The two old men talked together in low tones for a long time. Kahtahah could see that they were troubled. After the visitor left she went over to Snook and sat down beside him.

"What is troubling you, father?" she asked. "Has it anything to do with the strangers who came to the Great Raven House this afternoon?"

Snook called his household together.

"The strangers who came to the Raven house are kinsmen of the chief. The young man and woman both belong to the Raven clan and yet they have married each other. They have fled from their own village and are asking refuge among the Stikheenquan."

Everyone sat as though carved in stone. The strongest law of the Tlingit people! A member of the Raven clan MUST NOT marry another Raven. A Wolf MUST NOT marry a Wolf. It was as though a brother had married his sister.

No one spoke for a long time. A young man from the Great Raven House came to the door. "Our chief is calling a council at his house, and wishes the help of your advice."

Snook stood up and shook his head grimly. "Tell your chief I have no advice to give to the Raven clan. He knows how a chief of the Wolf clan punishes one who breaks the law."

Kahtahah shivered. She looked at Snook in wonder. Where was the kind father she had always known? This man who looked so grim and fierce filled her with fear. She remembered an old story that her foster mother had whispered to her. Long before she was born, when Snook was still a young and vigorous man, his niece had left his house to run away with one of her own clan. Snook had followed them and had brought back his niece. In the presence of his whole household he had condemned her to death for having broken the Tlingit law. He took her out with him in a canoe but returned alone. No one ever mentioned her name in his presence again.

Kahtahah shivered. This was the first time the story had seemed real to her.

Late that night the chief of the Great Raven House himself came to Snook's fireside. All evening while the council met to determine the fate of the young people, Snook had sat alone, silent and grim. The women of his household had not even dared to offer him food. The Raven chief sat down beside Snook, took out his box of leaf tobacco and offered it to him. The two old men smoked in silence for some time. Then the Raven chief spoke: "My kahnee (brother-in-law), my head is low. My grandchildren have broken the law. I have grown old and weak. The power of the white man is strong. I cannot fight the white man."

"So, the guilty ones will be protected in your house because the law of the white man is stronger than the law of the Tlingit," answered Snook. "What does the white man care about Tlingit law or Tlingit honor? It has always been the Tlingit law that a brother may not marry his sister."

"It is true that the law is an old one," the Raven chief said. "It's so old that we do not know the beginning. We Tlingits have many customs whose meaning we do not understand, and this law of the clans is such a one."

"We understand that a brother may not marry a sister," protested Snook.

"But there is no blood relationship between the young people," countered the Raven chief.

"It is still the law that they may not marry," Snook stubbornly maintained.

The old Raven chief stood up and drew his blanket tightly about him as he prepared to leave. "We have held our council, and we have decided. The times are changing. The white people are among us to stay, and if we break the law of the white people the captain of the gunboat will turn his guns on our village. Then the blood of our children and our grandchildren will be on our heads. How can the Tlingit fight the gunboat? We do not know, but perhaps the law of the white man is better than our law. We are willing to try the white man's way. The young people will have a home in my house. That is all."

Snook smoked another pipeful in silence after the Raven chief had gone. Then he spoke to his family. "If these young people had not been willful, this trouble would not have come to our people. Let all within the household beware of bringing disgrace to our name in this manner."

Kahtahah knew that Snook would never forgive one of his young people who had disobeyed the law of the clans and brought terrible disgrace to his name.

The Death of the Shaman

For several days everybody in the village watched the waters toward the west for the relatives of the young people, who were expected to come searching for them. Trouble was anticipated, but a week went by and no canoe had appeared. Gradually the excitement died down.

Word went around the village a short time later that the shaman, very old and almost blind, was making medicine. Shquindy was foretelling his own death, and named the day he would die. On that day he called his family around him and told them where he wished his burial house to be built. He chose the rattles and charms and other secret things that he wanted to be placed in the house with his body. The things he left behind were to be given to his successor, who would be recognized as having received Shquindy's spirit by the lock of light hair on the crown of his head.

Shquindy ordered his family to dress him in his full ceremonial shaman's costume. He lay down on his bed and closed his eyes, and when his nephews came to him in the morning he was dead. The sudden sound of loud wailing in the air gave notice to the village that the shaman was gone.

That night the Teehitton family invited the Wolf families of the village to a mourning feast, which was different from the pleasure feasts. There was no dancing, and tobacco was offered to all the guests. As they sat smoking the men rose to make speeches to comfort the dead man's family, and to tell tales of the great magic he had made in the days gone by; how he had driven away the witches from the sick; how he had helped the Stikheenquan in battle; how he had found the bodies of the drowned; and how he had brought wealth and power and fame to his clan.

The women of the Teehitton family sat on the ground rocking back and forth in grief, their heads bowed to their knees. Between speeches they lifted their voices high in thin mourning wails. Kahtahah wailed with the others because she belonged to the Teehitton family. At first she peeked through her long lashes to watch, but as the evening dragged on, the same stories repeated in speech after speech, she grew sleepy. She and Tsoonkla leaned against each other and went sound asleep.

She awoke hours later to hear Snook ending his speech: "Yes, yes, my grandfather, we remember you are mourning. It is not these guests here who are smoking the tobacco you have offered us. It is as if the spirits of our long dead uncles and grandfathers have been smoking with us. Do not mourn any longer. This uncle of yours is not dead. Your chief has seen your tears and has come back to wipe them away. That is the way it is."

Shquindy's nephew, who would succeed him as the head of his house, rose and replied, "I thank all of you deeply for the things you have done to these grandfathers of yours by your kind words. All of us, your grandfathers, were as if sick. But you are good medicine for us. Your words have cured us. Thank you, thank you."

Shquindy's orders were obeyed in every detail. Every article of medicine-making that he had named was collected. His body, still dressed in ceremonial garments, was placed in a large canoe for the journey to his last resting place. All the canoes of the village accompanied him to show how highly he was regarded.

They followed the route to the summer camp. For the site of his burial house, Shquindy had chosen an exposed headland a few miles beyond the halfway point from which one could see in every direction. Since he belonged to the Raven clan, only members of the Wolf clan could touch his body or perform any of the acts necessary for burial, even paddling the canoe that bore his body.

The hair of the Raven clan women was cut shoulder length as a sign of mourning, and their faces were streaked with black soot paint. Their voices wailed in weird, high-pitched sounds, which had continued without letup day and night ever since the shaman's death. There, at sunset, on the shore among the black hemlock trees, Kahtahah thought the wails sounded like the calls of some magic birds of the spirit world.

The young men quickly finished building the little burial house and the shaman's body was placed in it, surrounded by all the charms of his craft. The canoes started home, and the wailing ceased, replaced by laughter and joking. The next evening, at home, all of the Raven people were invited to a big feast at Snook's house to make them forget their grief. Valuable presents were distributed by Shquindy's family to all who had helped with the burial ceremonies. Not to have rewarded all who served in this way would have brought lasting shame to the Teehitton family.

Many years later the grave of Shquindy was disturbed. A white hunter found the ruins of the little burial house, long since broken down by the wind and the rain, and he eagerly scratched among the rotting boards and fallen leaves. He knew that gold bracelets and other articles were often found in old Indian graves and would bring good prices from curio dealers.

Kahtahah heard that a white man had offered some queerly carved bones that appeared to be shaman's charms to a curio dealer. She hunted up the white man, but he denied having robbed Shquindy's grave or having offered such things for sale. But that night, a paper box containing a large bundle of killer whale teeth, beaks of birds and other small bones used in the mysterious rites of a shaman was left at Kahtahah's front door. There was also a pair of carved cedar sticks, black with age, which Kahtahah remembered having seen Shquindy use many times when he was making medicine. Kahtahah gave these sticks to the son she had named Shquindy, and many times the new Shquindy used the old medicine man's sticks to beat the time for a Christian anthem or chorus in Alaskan villages.

Visitors from the Tsimshian Country

◆◆◆◆◆◆◆◆◆◆◆◆◆◆◆◆◆◆◆◆◆◆◆◆◆◆◆◆◆◆◆◆◆◆◆◆◆◆◆

There was great excitement on the beach one day shortly before the people left for spring eulachon camp. A large canoe of visitors—Christian Indians—had come from the Tsimshian country. A round of entertainment began at all the houses. The visitors sang new songs called church songs. There was no dancing!

In due time they made their errand known. They carried a message to Snook. An important man of the Tsimshians wished to marry Snook's daughter whom he had seen at the village of the Haidas. He was not a young man, but he had an established position and wealth. Now that he had become a Christian and given up the old customs, there was no danger that he would make himself poor by giving feasts. He sent, however, gifts to Snook in the old style, but, equally important to the Indians, he belonged to the Eagle clan.

The messengers said that he nevertheless did not intend to marry in the Indian style. He requested that the young woman accompany his friends to his country, where the Christian missionary would marry them in the way of the church and the law.

Snook had grown more and more attached to the Tlingit ways as he grew older. He did not understand the white man's God, and did not like the white man's law any better than he liked the white man's liquor. With great dignity he thanked the visitors for the honor accorded his family, but he said his foster daughter was still a child and had no thought of marriage.

All of the chiefs and elders of the nine other Great Houses in the village begged Snook to change his mind. From early morning until late at night they sat around the center fire in Snook's house and

talked, presenting, as they rose one by one, the good reasons for
the marriage. They reminded Snook of his age and the old wounds
in his legs; they spoke of the changing times, and of the evil white
men who were passing up and down the Stikine in the gold rush;
they praised the position and the wealth of the Tsimshian man;
they talked of the great honor offered the Stikheenquan; and they
praised the beauty and the modest behavior of Kahtahah.

The next day they again gathered to convince Snook of the
wisdom of the marriage. Snook's wife took no public part in the
talk, but she sat by his side and listened to the speeches of the
elders. She often expressed agreement in a low voice meant only
for his ears. After another long, weary day, Snook at last yielded
and gave his promise.

96

He called Kahtahah from the shadows far from the fire and spoke solemnly to her. "My daughter, I know that you do not wish to marry. But you have heard the strong talk that has been made to me by my friends. Bitter as it is for me to say it, the talk is true. This will be a good marriage for you.

"It is not as if you are going among strangers. You know that many of the Stikine chiefs carry Tsimshian names that they earned in warfare long ago. It is not so with the name of your mother's family. Your chief also carries a Tsimshian name, but by birth. So you will find your own people among the Tsimshians. I give you to them to guard."

Gifts were presented to Snook in the name of the absent suitor. The frightened Kahtahah was placed in the canoe in the care of one of their women, and the visitors set out on the long paddle homeward. It was a travel-stained and sullen Kahtahah who walked up the Tsimshian beach one week later. She had picked up a few words of the strange Tsimshian language during the trip, but not for worlds would she have admitted that she understood anything. The high nasal sound of their talk wearied her since her ears were tuned to the low guttural tones of the Tlingit. The Tsimshian women looked at her with curiosity. They thought she was older than she really was because she was so tall. She kept her head down in the manner of a well-trained

Tlingit girl, but she knew they were staring at her and talking about her. Only her pride kept her from crying aloud.

Finally a young Tlingit woman, who had lived with the Tsimshians for many years, came to her. She secretly hated to have the rich Tsimshian chief go so far from home to choose a wife.

"It is said that you do not wish to marry this chief. Can this be true?" she asked.

"I don't want to marry anyone," Kahtahah answered.

"He is a rich man, and no longer spends his money on feasts. He will be kind to you. Many women have wished to marry this chief," said the young woman.

"I don't want to marry anyone," Kahtahah said again.

"Have you heard that we are Christian Indians here? We have given up the old customs, so if you do not wish to marry this man, no one can force you to," suggested the young woman.

When the chief heard what Kahtahah had said, he sent word that he would not force her to marry him if she refused him before the council. That evening all of the people in the village had a meeting. The missionary who was teaching them about the Christian God was present. Kahtahah sat quietly while the man who wished to be her husband spoke to her through an interpreter.

"It is said that you have come to our village unwillingly; that you do not wish to marry me. Although I have given your people many presents, I do not care about that. But I must hear from your own mouth what you wish to do."

Kahtahah's heart beat wildly. She stood up, but her knees would hardly hold her. "Who will help me?" she thought. "It is no use to ask the Raven for help. I will ask the white man's God to make me strong." Courage came to her, and she lifted her head and spoke clearly, "I do not wish to marry any man."

Then the missionary stood up. "It is plain that this girl is very young. Let me take her to my home. My wife will take care of her and perhaps in time she will change her mind about marrying."

All the Tsimshian elders nodded their heads in agreement.

"That is best. That is wise," they said.

So Kahtahah went to live in the mission house.

The Mission House

Another Indian girl lived in the mission house, and as soon as Kahtahah began to understand her language she became happy. She learned English very quickly, and without thinking, the right English word often came to her lips.

She was taught to make her bed and to use a knife and fork and small spoon. She learned that she should eat only from her own plate and not from the common bowl. She watched the other girl, who had been there longer, and copied her ways. Her worst trouble was learning to comb her long, thick hair neatly every day. Sometimes the other girl laughed loudly at her mistakes. Kahtahah's eyes would blaze in anger, and it took many of the missionary's kind words and diplomatic skills to keep peace.

Kahtahah helped the missionary plant a garden. She carried baskets full of small rocks away so that only the fine earth was left and hauled pails of water for the seeds.

One day she heard the sound of Tlingit words and was suddenly homesick. Tears rolled down her face. Though the man who spoke was a stranger, she asked him to take her home to Snook and her foster mother. The man was acquainted with people of her village and promised to help her. He told her to slip away from the mission house late that night and come to the beach where the canoes were lying. When the noises in the village had died down, she climbed out of the window with the help of the other girl and went to the beach. The man was not there, and she never learned why he did not come. She later thought it was because he feared trouble with the Tsimshians if he helped her.

She wandered along the beach among the canoes until she found one that she could push into the water. She had decided to go home all by herself. Never in her life had she held a paddle in her hand, since the slaves or the men of her family had always done that kind of work. But she took up the paddle and started on the long journey back to her own people, just as her mother had done. She paddled and paddled until it seemed she had gone miles. Dawn was coming when she finally came to an island. She was tired and the canoe was leaking, so she landed and climbed up on the rocks, where she found a sandy hollow and lay down and went to sleep. She had not fastened the canoe and when the tide came it floated away.

Meanwhile at breakfast the missionary discovered that Kahtahah was missing. The other girl confessed to having helped her out the window. The missionary gave the alarm in the village. The men found that a small canoe was gone, and searchers went out on the water in every direction. Someone found the empty canoe floating back toward the town with the rising tide. Everyone believed that Kahtahah had drowned.

The searchers in one canoe landed on the little island, and a man climbing the rocks to look out over the water found Kahtahah, still fast asleep. They took her back to the mission house unharmed by her little trip. She had paddled all of 5 of the 300 miles to home.

Kahtahah's Return

♦♦♦♦♦♦♦♦♦♦♦♦♦♦♦♦♦♦♦♦♦♦♦♦♦♦♦♦♦♦♦♦♦♦♦♦♦♦♦

Word came to Snook back in the village of the Stikheenquan that his foster daughter was a slave. She had been seen carrying loads and working in the white man's garden. Snook felt very sad. It was not fitting that one of Kahtahah's blood should work in that manner. Her grandmother and her great-grandmother had been high. None had been higher than they.

Snook sent a messenger with money to the missionary asking him to send Kahtahah home, but the missionary refused and sent this message back to Snook: "I have saved Kahtahah from one marriage when she was too young. You would only marry her to someone else. She is better off in my home."

That summer the soldiers came in the gunboat and landed on the beach beyond the point. They built a fort because more gold miners were coming into the Stikine country and trouble was expected. In the fall when Snook returned from beaver trapping he found something else new in the village. A missionary lady had come, and the soldiers at the fort had let her use one of their big buildings for a school. She was looking for little Indian girls to live in her house and go to her school.

Snook talked with his wife. "If Kahtahah must be taught the ways of the white people it is better that she should be near us."

So he sent two messages to the Tsimshian country, one to the chief who wished to marry Kahtahah, and the other to the missionary. To the chief he said, "Snook is returning gift for gift. Release my daughter from this marriage and send her home"; and to the missionary he said, "If you will send Kahtahah to her own people, we will give her to the missionary lady who has come to our village."

The missionary was an understanding man. He saw that Kahtahah would never willingly marry the Tsimshian chief, and that she was homesick for her own people. He placed her on a sailing ship that was leaving for the North on a trading voyage, and the captain promised to stop at the Stikine village.

Kahtahah was afraid. The only white man she knew was the missionary, who had seemed just like her foster father, and she had never been in any boat but a canoe. She locked herself in her little cabin of the white man's big sailing ship and would not open the door even for the captain.

At last one of the sailors spoke to her through the door in the Tlingit language. How good it sounded! He told her that she had nothing to fear from the white men, and to open the door so they could give her some food. Kahtahah was very hungry by this time and the thought of food, expressed in words of her own tongue, was tempting. She unlocked the door, and the sailor gave her an apple. It was the first apple she had ever eaten.

Three weeks later the ship reached the Stikine village, and long before they arrived, Kahtahah had forgotten her fear of the strange white men. But she never forgot the kind sailor who gave her her first apple.

School

◆◆◆◆◆◆◆◆◆◆◆◆◆◆◆◆◆◆◆◆◆◆◆◆◆◆◆◆◆◆◆◆◆◆◆◆

Snook kept his promise and took Kahtahah to the missionary lady. Kahtahah was eager to go to school. She lived there for three years, learning to read and write well and to sew and care for small children.

Soon after she started school, a missionary minister and his wife came to the village. They brought white man's lumber on a sailing ship and built a white church on the hill near the school. Every Sunday he told the people about God, the great Chief-on-high, who created the Tlingits as well as the other people of the world. At first he could not make the people understand because he could not talk the Tlingit language. He sent for an interpreter from a village farther south, but after a while he noticed how well Kahtahah spoke English. Therefore, he taught her to be his interpreter. Every Saturday they studied the words he would say on Sunday morning, and Kahtahah stood by his side in the pulpit with her head up like a white woman's, saying the minister's words in Tlingit so that all the people could hear.

When Snook first saw his foster daughter standing up before the people in this public fashion he was greatly ashamed and bowed his head as he listened to Kahtahah speaking in a loud voice. But in time he grew used to the sight and secretly was very proud of the high honor given one of his family. He and his wife never missed a service. It was his only contact with Kahtahah, because as long as she lived at the school she was not allowed to

visit Snook at his Great House. But he was content because he could see that she was in safe hands. Kahtahah was not bold, but she was brave. She thought that the minister was a very wise and good man, but she also thought that some of his teachings were not right for the people; for instance, one of his favorite stories about God, the great Chief-on-high, who was a good shepherd who went out into the mountains to rescue his sheep that were lost. He liked to say, "The Lord is my Shepherd, I shall not want. He maketh me to lie down in green pastures. . . ."

But Kahtahah said, "It does not sound right to tell the people that. I cannot say it so that it will sound right. Tlingits don't know about these pet sheep you tell about. They know only the wild mountain sheep, and they do not want a shepherd. They leap and run if they see a man. A wild mountain sheep can kill a wolf. The people will think me foolish if I tell them the great Chief-on-high will take care of them as a shepherd takes care of the wild mountain sheep!"

At another time the minister was reading about the great flood from the Bible, and how the windows of Heaven opened and the waters poured out, covering the whole world: "And the rain was upon the earth 40 days and 40 nights."

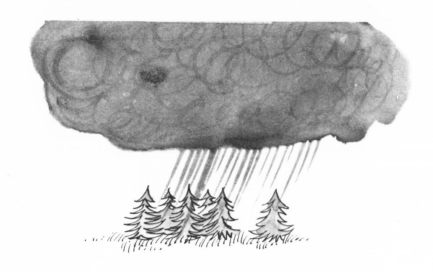

When he finished that verse, Kahtahah did not translate it into Tlingit. The minister, thinking that she had not understood, read it again, but still Kahtahah did not translate. The minister asked her, "Don't you understand, Kahtahah? It rained 40 days and 40 nights and the waters covered the earth."

Kahtahah's face was white but she spoke bravely. "I cannot tell the people that because they will not respect your Bible. It has often rained 40 days and 40 nights among us and no waters have covered the earth."

The minister looked at the young face turned so bravely toward him, and thought about the rain pouring down out of the sky on the Stikine village in the fall and springtime. He said no more about translating, and continued to read from the Bible.

Romance

◆◆◆◆◆◆◆◆◆◆◆◆◆◆◆◆◆◆◆◆◆◆◆◆◆◆◆◆◆◆◆◆◆

One early fall day when Kahtahah was 16, the teachers of the mission gave a picnic a few miles down the side of the island at Old Town. From the villagers they borrowed large canoes, which some of the young Indian men offered to paddle.

Kahtahah was in charge of a group of smaller children. One of the paddlers in her canoe was a young man, a stranger. He had come down the Stikine, where he had panned gold all summer, and was visiting his aunt until he could return home to the Tongass country on a passing trading ship.

The young man, Yeileenuk, looked at the tall young girl with her great brown eyes and sweet mouth and found her very beautiful. Before his gaze her cheeks flushed red, and he tried in vain to catch her eye. She was not only very shy, but a well-trained Tlingit girl. At last he spoke to her in English, "Will you hand me a drink of water, please?"

Kahtahah gave him the water, but her hand shook so much that she spilled many drops. The young man smiled. But Kahtahah still did not say a word.

The next day the young man called at the mission and told the teachers that he wished to marry Kahtahah. The teachers were not surprised. They asked him many questions and learned that he had gone to a mission school and could read and write even better than Kahtahah. They sent for his aunt and talked with them both again. They were pleased with the young man and told him he could speak to Kahtahah.

Kahtahah thought of her kind foster father. She knew all the Tlingit customs and said, "You must speak to Snook. I want him to be satisfied."

Her lover laughed. "Since you wish it, I will speak to Snook, but I will not give presents for you in the Tlingit style. We are white people now. I gave up the old customs long ago!"

Yeileenuk went to see Snook in his Great House in the curve of the bay. The old man's eyes were still as keen as those of the hawk that swoops down on the little sawbill duck. The young man seemed pleasing to him, tall and strong and open-faced. His manner was respectful.

"What is your Tlingit name?" the old man asked.

"Yeileenuk" (Raven's prying beak).

"A high name! The Wolf clan. Your grandfather has given many feasts. Come near," said Snook.

The young man stepped closer. Snook stood up and felt the lobes of his ears. "One, two, three, four holes," he said. "Four feasts in your honor. That is well." What he meant was that he was pleased with the clan and caste of Kahtahah's lover.

But Yeileenuk laughed. "Those holes in my ears were put there when I was too small to object. My grandfather has given four more feasts since then, but I would not let them make any more holes in my ears. I have given up all that folly."

A month later Kahtahah and Yeileenuk were married by the minister with the words of the Christian faith, "Until death do us part!"

In his Great House in the curve of the bay Snook was troubled. He could not understand the young people, although the marriage seemed to promise well. The young man had been respectful and had conformed to the Tlingit customs in the beginning, but no gifts had come from his people to Kahtahah's family. It would not be a real marriage unless the proper respect were shown to the family of the bride.

"What are a few words out of a little black book in the hands of the minister? Words! Words! Anyone can say words, but presents are different. Presents are a sign of something lasting," Snook told his wife sadly.

The Old Custom Wins

◆◆◆◆◆◆◆◆◆◆◆◆◆◆◆◆◆◆◆◆◆◆◆◆◆◆◆◆◆◆◆◆◆◆◆◆

Up in the north on the Chilkat River was a village of fierce and proud Tlingits, where the word of the shaman was still strong. The people believed that they got sick and died because someone had bewitched them. The white people were afraid of the Tlingits in this village.

The minister felt that only the power contained in the Bible could drive out the shaman, and so he asked Yeileenuk and Kahtahah to go there and open a school. He knew that the family names of Yeileenuk and Kahtahah were so high that they would be welcome and safe among those wild and cruel people.

The great chief Shotkitch welcomed them, calling Yeileenuk "my son" because Shotkitch had been married to a woman from the Stikine village of Snook's tribe. He gave them land for their school, and all the young men of the Raven clan helped to build a log cabin before the cold northern winter set in.

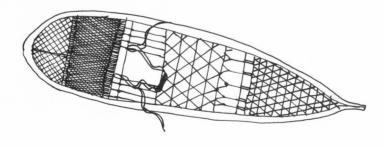

The Chilkat country was very different from Kahtahah's home. She learned to walk on snowshoes and made more than one trip all the way to the mouth of the river where the trading vessel had left their supplies. In the winter she watched the men cut holes in the thick ice and spear big king salmon for fresh food.

The next year Yeileenuk took Kahtahah down to the Tongass country to visit his own people. His grandfather, who was old and did not have long to live, wished to see his grandson before he died and give him a message in person.

"My grandson," the old chief said, "I have grown old and feeble, but I am still a great chief. You are white people now, you say. Perhaps that is well. But I am Tlingit; my name is high, and I wish to keep it high. I want you to go north and take a present from me to Snook. I have sent for a new canoe from the Haidas."

Yeileenuk was very gentle with his old grandfather. He did not laugh.

"I understand, my grandfather," he said. "Your heart is low because you think I have brought disgrace to your name by taking my wife in the style of the white people. When we go back to the village of the Stikines to show Snook his new little grandson we will take the Haida canoe."

"All winter long the Haida canoe maker worked on the red cedar log, fashioning the graceful lines of the Haida canoe. It was painted from bow to stern in bold Eagle designs. It was not as large as the old Eagle canoe in which Kahtahah had made so many journeys, but it was easier to handle and faster.

In the spring Yeileenuk and Kahtahah and the new little brown baby traveled to the Stikine village in a trading vessel. They took the new canoe with them. After it was unloaded from the ship, Yeileenuk called four young men who were to him as nephews in the Eagle clan and asked them to try out the canoe. They paddled in fine style, back and forth on the water in front of Snook's Great House. They dug their paddles deep into the water, lifting the canoe forward in great leaps, shouting as if they were racing. They could feel that it was a fast canoe.

Everybody of the village watched from the shore. They knew that this was a matter of great importance to the old Tlingit chief.

At last, with a skillful thrust of his steering paddle, Yeileenuk turned the canoe toward the beach in front of Snook's house as the happy young men gave their paddles a final flip that is known only to experts. They then stopped the canoe with powerful backward strokes, and turning the canoe around, came to the beach, stern first. Tlingits always beached their fine Haida canoes stern first so as not to injure the sharp knife edge of the bow.

Yeileenuk dropped the steering paddle and stepped out of the canoe. He walked up to Snook, who stood before the door of his Great House in sight of all the village.

"Your nephew has brought you a present. It is really nothing very much. It is a gift from my grandfather. We wish it were more," he said in a small voice, as if it were a matter of no importance.

Snook answered, "Your grandfather is a high chief. He honors me. It is the finest canoe in the village."

Then he turned to the women of his house and said, "Prepare food. Invite the people. The husband of my daughter eats with me."

The proud old Tlingit chief drew himself erect, tall and imposing. This was a language that he understood. This was according to the good old Tlingit customs. This was not the foolish way of the white man.

Not in vain had he taught his beloved daughter. She had been true to her Tlingit honor.

Paul, Frances Lackey, 1889-1970.
    Kahtahah / Frances Lackey Paul ; illustrated
by Rie Muñoz.   Anchorage, Alaska Northwest Pub.
Co., c1976.
    ix, 109p. illus. 27cm.

    Summary: Draws on the experiences of a real
person to recreate the life of a Tlingit Indian
girl of nineteenth-century Alaska.

1.Tlingit Indians. 2.Indians of North America-Alaska.
I.Muñoz, Rie. II.Title.